GUILDFORD BRANCH

As one of the world's longest established
and best-known travel brands,
Thomas Cook are the experts in travel.

For more than 135 years our
guidebooks have unlocked the secrets
of destinations around the world,
sharing with travellers a wealth of
experience and a passion for travel.

**Rely on Thomas Cook as your
travelling companion on your next trip
and benefit from our unique heritage.**

W9-BGE-133

Thomas Cook **pocket** guides

VANCOUVER

Charlene Rooke

Your travelling companion since 1873

Written by Charlene Rooke

Published by Thomas Cook Publishing
A division of Thomas Cook Tour Operations Limited
Company registration No: 3772199 England
The Thomas Cook Business Park, 9 Coningsby Road
Peterborough PE3 8SB, United Kingdom
Email: books@thomascook.com, Tel: +44 (0)1733 416477
www.thomascookpublishing.com

Produced by The Content Works Ltd
Aston Court, Kingsmead Business Park, Frederick Place
High Wycombe, Bucks HP11 1LA
www.thecontentworks.com

Series design based on an original concept by Studio 183 Limited

ISBN: 978-1-84848-292-0

First edition © 2010 Thomas Cook Publishing
Text © Thomas Cook Publishing
Maps © Thomas Cook Publishing/PCGraphics (UK) Limited
Transport map © Communicarta Limited

Series Editor: Lucy Armstrong
Production/DTP: Steven Collins

Printed and bound in Spain by GraphyCems

Cover photography (Totem Pole in Stanley Park) © Armand-Photo-Travel/Alamy

All rights reserved. No part of this publication may be reproduced, stored in a retrieval system or transmitted, in any form or any means, electronic, mechanical, recording or otherwise, in any part of the world, without prior permission of the publisher. Requests for permission should be made to the publisher at the above address.

Although every care has been taken in compiling this publication, and the contents are believed to be correct at the time of printing, Thomas Cook Tour Operations Limited cannot accept any responsibility for errors or omission, however caused, or for changes in details given in the guidebook, or for the consequences of any reliance on the information provided. Descriptions and assessments are based on the author's views and experiences when writing and do not necessarily represent those of Thomas Cook Tour Operations Limited.

CONTENTS

INTRODUCING VANCOUVER
Introduction...................6
When to go....................8
Stanley Park..................12
History........................14
Lifestyle......................16
Culture........................18

MAKING THE MOST OF VANCOUVER
Shopping......................22
Eating & drinking.............24
Entertainment & nightlife.....28
Sport & relaxation............30
Accommodation................32
The best of Vancouver.........38
Suggested itineraries.........40
Something for nothing.........42
When it rains.................44
On arrival....................46

THE CITY OF VANCOUVER
Downtown......................58
West Side.....................74
East Side.....................90

OUT OF TOWN TRIPS
Whistler......................104
Victoria......................116

PRACTICAL INFORMATION
Directory.....................128
Emergencies...................138

INDEX.........................140

MAPS
Vancouver.....................48
Vancouver transport map.......52
Downtown......................60
West Side.....................76
East Side.....................92
Around Vancouver..............106

SYMBOLS KEY

The following symbols are used throughout this book:

@ address ☎ telephone ⓦ website address
🕐 opening times Ⓝ public transport connections

The following symbols are used on the maps:

ℹ️	information office	▦	points of interest
✈	airport	O	city
✚	hospital	O	large town
🛡	police station	○	small town
🚍	bus station	=	motorway
🚆	railway station	—	main road
Ⓜ	SkyTrain	—	minor road
✝	church	—	railway
❶	numbers denote featured cafés & restaurants		

Hotels and restaurants are graded by approximate price as follows:
£ budget price **££** mid-range price **£££** expensive

Abbreviations used in this guide:

St   Street
Rd   Road
Ave   Avenue
b/n   between

◉ *View of Downtown from Stanley Park*

INTRODUCING
Vancouver

Introduction

Welcome to Canada's Lotusland, as locals like to call Vancouver – a West Coast playground that could easily be a cousin of US cities like Seattle, Portland or San Francisco. It's an anomaly within Canada, a city that escapes northern winter and stays blissfully snow-free all year round. Its geography is equally blessed: it has a stunning location tucked between mountains and the ocean, and is both close to the US border and a gateway to the Pacific Rim. Vancouverites are friendly and polite in the Canadian way, yet laid-back in uniquely West Coast style. All these factors make Vancouver one of the most liveable, likeable cities in the world.

Many of Vancouver's residents were not born in the city, but arrived from elsewhere and decided to stay. Not a few of the fleece-clad newcomers are drawn by the beaches, the world-class cycling and skiing in the area and the eco-friendly lifestyle – this is

the city that spawned Greenpeace in 1971. A wave of new immigrants and investment flowed into Vancouver from Hong Kong around the time of its handover to China in 1997, and as a consequence Vancouver has taken on a strong pan-Asian character. Thousands of Korean, Japanese and Taiwanese immigrants and students now call the city home, bringing with them a taste for everything from luxury designer goods and soaring glass towers to *izakaya* restaurants.

When the sun shines, Vancouver is a paradise on earth. Just wait for winter's deluge; there's a reason it's nicknamed Rain City. But the city blooms to life once again in spring, with a riot of hydrangeas, lilacs, magnolias and cherry and apple blossoms. Rollerbladers and joggers colonise the city's seawall paths, sailboats and yachts venture out from the marinas, and patios fill up with coffee- and cocktail-drinking crowds. Vancouver is the girl next door of cities: fresh, natural, unaffected and all too easy to fall in love with.

Panorama of False Creek and English Bay

When to go

Vancouver has a temperate climate, making a visit enjoyable at any time of year. Summer in particular is a magical season, when toned and tanned Vancouverites don sandals and flip-flops to enjoy sunny days and late sunsets at the beach. If you don't like rain, on the other hand, avoid coming in winter.

SEASONS & CLIMATE

Temperatures in December and January can dip to 0°C (32°F), but any snow usually melts as it hits the ground. At all times of year, have an umbrella handy, because this city stays lush and green through an average 120 cm (47 in) of precipitation annually. In June, July and August the weather is at its best, with long days and temperatures as high as 30°C (86°F), but beaches, attractions and shopping areas are packed with holidaymakers. May, September and October are the perfect times to visit, being sunny and crowd-free.

ANNUAL EVENTS
January & February

Polar Bear Swim Since 1920, up to 2,000 brave swimmers have plunged into English Bay on New Year's Day for a refreshing start to the year. Joining them is optional.

Chinese New Year The city's Chinese community celebrates with parades, performances and feasts. ⓦ www.vancouverchinatown.ca

Winterruption Family activities, arts workshops and performances on Granville Island help to warm up the end of February. ⓦ www.granvilleisland.com

March & April

Vancouver Playhouse International Wine Festival Wineries run tasting booths at the Vancouver Convention & Exhibition Centre in late March or April. Ⓦ www.playhousewinefest.com

Sun Run This fun, easy 10 km (6.3 mile) race at the end of April is always popular. Ⓦ www.vancouversun.com

May & June

Night Markets Between May and September, visit the night markets for Hong Kong-style street eats and bargain merchandise. Ⓐ Keefer St, b/n Main & Columbia Sts Ⓦ www.vcma.shawbiz.ca

Bard on the Beach From May to September, four classic plays are staged in tents in Vanier Park. Ⓦ www.bardonthebeach.org

🔺 *Canada Day fireworks display in Vancouver's Downtown*

Vancouver International Children's Festival Face paints, puppets and sing-alongs at this outdoor festival in Vanier Park in late May. ⓦ www.childrensfestival.ca

Rio Tinto Alcan Dragon Boat Festival Nearly 100,000 people line False Creek to watch June's dragon boat races, with food, entertainment and viewing centred around the Plaza of Nations. ⓦ www.dragonboatbc.ca

Kitsilano Showboat Since 1935, the concert bowl above Kitsilano Pool has featured an eclectic line-up of young dancers, community bands and old-timey entertainers every Monday, Wednesday and Friday night between June and August. ⓦ www.kitsilanoshowboat.com

July & August

TD Canada Trust Vancouver International Jazz Festival An accessible mix of jazz, blues and urban music, held at the beginning of July. ⓦ www.coastaljazz.ca

Theatre Under the Stars Musical Society Perky, quirky summer performances of Broadway's best at Malkin Bowl outdoor theatre in Stanley Park. ⓦ www.tuts.ca

Vancouver Folk Music Festival In late July, chill out at Jericho Beach Park listening to the good vibrations of folk, country and world music. ⓦ www.thefestival.bc.ca

HSBC Celebration of Light Stunning fireworks, synchronised to classical music, over English Bay at the end of July. ⓦ www.celebration-of-light.com

Pride Week The gay community comes out in early August for a week of entertainment and a colourful family-friendly parade through the West End. ⓦ www.vancouverpride.ca

September & October

Vancouver International Fringe Festival An independent spirit infuses street performances, plays and art offerings on and around Granville Island in early September. ⓦ www.vancouverfringe.com

Vancouver International Film Festival Focusing on world cinema, this popular festival in October screens 350 films from 60 countries. ⓦ www.viff.org

November & December

Stanley Park Christmas Train A vintage miniature railway chugs along past charmingly homespun holiday displays during November and December. ⓦ www.vancouver.ca

Santa Claus Parade At the beginning of December, a colourful parade to get you into the Christmas spirit. ⓦ www.rogerssantaclausparade.com

PUBLIC HOLIDAYS

New Year's Day 1 Jan

Good Friday 2 Apr 2010, 22 Apr 2011, 6 Apr 2012

Victoria Day 24 May 2010, 23 May 2011, 21 May 2012

Canada Day 1 July

BC Day 2 Aug 2010, 1 Aug 2011, 6 Aug 2012

Labour Day 6 Sept 2010, 5 Sept 2011, 3 Sept 2012

Thanksgiving Day 11 Oct 2010, 10 Oct 2011, 8 Oct 2012

Remembrance Day 11 Nov

Christmas Day 25 Dec

Stanley Park

Vancouver's green lung is a huge urban park with an area of 1,000 acres (400 hectares). Created around 1888, Stanley Park is one of the defining features of this sporty, outdoors-oriented, healthy city that regularly appears on lists of the world's best places to live. While locals revel in the recreational opportunities, which include a popular seawall trail for running, biking and rollerblading, plus a nine-hole golf course and extensive hiking trails, visitors flock here for its stunning vantage points like Prospect Point and family attractions like the farmyard-style zoo and aquarium.

Dining options range from casual takeaway joints to fine dining restaurants – the Fish House (see page 27) is one of Vancouver's best places to eat. As a touchstone for locals and visitors alike, Stanley Park has inspired artists, authors (including Timothy Taylor, with his award-winning culinary novel *Stanley Park*) and countless generations of Vancouverites, especially those who live in the adjacent West End residential area.

In the winter of 2006–7, a devastating wind storm damaged more than 10 per cent of the Stanley Park forest, downing 10,000 trees and significantly changing the visual profile of the park. Vancouverites responded with an outpouring of grief and generosity that has resulted in 16,000 new trees being planted there. Likewise, for years debate has raged about the so-called Hollow Tree, a park attraction for more than a century. The Hollow Tree is basically a dead stump of a massive red cedar, estimated to be 700 years old, and big enough for a car to drive through it. Though it also received hard knocks from the same storm and now leans at an angle much like the Leaning Tower of Pisa, any city engineers who attempt to cut it down face angry protests from locals – such is the love of Vancouverites for their Stanley Park, and every living thing in it.

⬢ Totem poles in Stanley Park

History

Vancouver could easily have been called Narvaez or Galiano, since Spanish explorers José María Narváez and Dionisio Alcalá Galiano were among the first Europeans to set anchor near here. (The Coast Salish aboriginal people had, in truth, already been here for thousands of years.) But the glory all went to Captain George Vancouver, who arrived in 1792 while exploring the West Coast and the Pacific.

It wasn't until the 1820s that a Hudson's Bay Company trading post opened at what was then called Fort Vancouver, and not until the 1850s that the first wave of visitors arrived in British Columbia – not Americans in search of cheap exchange-rate shopping, but adventurers in search of the gold that had been discovered in the Fraser River. In 1867, 'Gassy' Jack Deighton established a key landmark: Vancouver's first saloon, in the port area after which the Gastown nightlife district is still named. The city was inaugurated in 1886, the same year that it was almost completely destroyed by a fire but resiliently rose from the ashes.

In the late 19th and early 20th centuries, two major parks were created: much of what is now Pacific Spirit Regional Park near the University of British Columbia, and Stanley Park on the west side of the Downtown peninsula. The precursors of the bridges that still define the city's geography today – Granville (1889), Cambie (1912), Second Narrows (1925), Burrard (1932) and Lions Gate (1938) – began to rise.

Though Victoria has always been the capital of British Columbia, Vancouver quickly became its major shipping hub and residential area. It didn't have quite as much luck as a financial centre: the Vancouver Stock Exchange, founded in 1907, endured a series of scandals and frauds and was eventually merged into the Canadian Venture Exchange in 1999.

Vancouver has always been a city of village-like neighbourhoods. Canada's late 19th-century railway boom brought Chinese workers to Vancouver, who settled in what is now North America's third-largest Chinatown (after New York and San Francisco). The former factory and sawmill hub once known as Industrial Island is now the Granville Island Public Market, surrounded by waterside condominium homes. What started as a brickworks in the backwoods of the city has become the densely populated West End. Today's chic Yaletown rose in the last 20 years from disused warehouses and train yards. And from its roots as a counter-culture hippie enclave in the 1960s, Kitsilano has turned into a sophisticated and highly desirable urban address.

Vancouver has proved well able to host high-profile, large-scale, global events, including the Expo world fair in 1986, the year of the city's centenary, and the Winter Olympic Games in February 2010. The Olympics have boosted investment and infrastructure in the city and region, with the opening of the new SkyTrain Canada Line and improvements on Highway 99 to Whistler. The athletes' village provides a cluster of new housing units – some of them public or affordable housing – and the purpose-built convention centre and cross-country ski and speed-skating facilities will bring many more tourists and businesses to Vancouver in the future. Yet despite springing up so quickly from an original settlement of a thousand people to a sophisticated metropolis of more than two million residents, Vancouver has managed to grow into a major city with the feel of a small and friendly town.

Lifestyle

Some cities live to work, while others work to live. Vancouverites are itching to don their fleece or Lycra and hit the slopes, hiking and biking trails or pool as soon as possible. Outside the business centre, it's common for workdays to have a leisurely start, with casually dressed employees reluctantly trickling out of coffee shops around 09.00, morning brew – in an eco-friendly cup, of course – in hand. Avid bands of urban cyclists (watch out!) commute across the bridges that connect Vancouver's Downtown to the North Shore and Lower Mainland. At lunchtime, joggers sweat in the city parks and streets. By 17.00 on a summer Friday, good luck finding anyone still at work!

Vancouverites tend to eat, shop and socialise close to home – there's no confusing a chic Yaletown socialite with a granola-fed Kitsilano yuppie. That means that wherever you are, there's bound to be a host of great neighbourhood bars and boutiques, quietly humming every night of the week. While Thursday, Friday and Saturday are buzz-worthy nights for dancing and live music, Sundays are quiet.

At weekends, the streets of stylish enclaves fill with expensive baby strollers pushed by young parents dressed in designer athletic gear and clutching non-fat lattes and recycled-cloth sacks filled with organic groceries. Expect a slower pace, both on the sidewalks and on the streets. There's no point in trying to jaywalk, for instance. Vancouver drivers are so polite, cars will actually stop to let you cross!

A frustration of daily life in a water-bound city is bridge traffic. In particular, the Lions Gate, the architecturally charming but often bottle-necked bridge that joins Downtown to the North Shore, jams up during rush hour and weekends. (Pay close attention to lane control lights overhead, see page 51). If you find yourself fuming behind a big SUV or a double-wide stroller, just chill out and enjoy the scenery. That's what the locals do.

🔺 *Cyclists wind their way along the False Creek seawall path*

Culture

Vancouver has earned its place in the international canon on a number of cultural fronts. The Vancouver School of photography started a wave of photorealism 20 years ago that has sparked a lively street-art scene and still packs out city galleries (see page 65). On the architecture front, Vancouverism is becoming a globally known genre, characterised by tall apartment towers on stubby bases. Archi-tourists will want to take a walk past the public buildings of the 'concrete poet', the late Vancouver architect Arthur Erickson, that dot Downtown, particularly the **Robson Square complex** (ⓦ www.arthurericksonconservancy.com). Also take in the impressive, coliseum-shaped Vancouver Public Library (see page 64) by famed Canadian architect Moshe Safdie.

The home town of artists from Bryan Adams to Sarah McLachlan still has a vibrant live music scene in the vintage theatres, clubs and bars lining the neon alley of Granville Street, in Downtown. In particular, don't miss a chance to see the opulent interior of the **Orpheum Theatre** (ⓐ 601 Smithe St ⓣ 604-665-3050 ⓦ www.city.vancouver.bc.ca/theatres ⓝ Bus: 4, 6, 7, 10, 16, 17, 50), perhaps during a performance of the **Vancouver Symphony Orchestra** (ⓣ 604-876-3434 ⓦ www.vancouversymphony.ca).

For live theatre fans, Granville Island is the place to be, with a handful of resident companies including two Arts Club Theatre venues (see page 81) and the Vancouver TheatreSports League (see page 82) improvisation troupe. The Waterfront Theatre and **Performance Works** groups (ⓣ 604-687-3005

🔺 *Vancouver Art Gallery by night*

WHAT'S ON?

Local culture vultures consult the *Westender* and the *Georgia Straight* for weekly events listings. The monthly *Vancouver* magazine also offers a thoughtful, well-edited selection. For many cultural events, half-price tickets are available on performance day from the **Tickets Tonight** (ⓐ 200 Burrard St ⓣ 604-684-2787 ⓦ www.ticketstonight.ca ⓣ 10.00–18.00 Mon–Sat) booth in the Tourism Vancouver Visitor Centre (see page 137).

ⓦ www.giculturalsociety.org) are based in funky industrial spaces.

If you're booking your trip through an accredited travel agent, be sure to ask for a free Tourism Vancouver Attraction Pass, which includes free admission for two people to dozens of museums, gardens and other places of interest. A Smartvisit Card is also a worthwhile investment, offering free admission to more than 50 local sites. You can buy the latter card online at ⓦ www.seevancouvercard.com.

▶ *Family-favourite Science World and its geodesic dome (see page 134)*

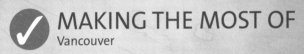

MAKING THE MOST OF
Vancouver

Shopping

The real shopping scores in Vancouver are products conceived in the city. Comfy, bright yoga gear has become ubiquitous apparel since local line Lululemon (see opposite) started making its famously flattering stretch pants in 2000. Supply Cosmetics was founded here, and its products are still sold at the girly BeautyMark (see page 66) boutique in Yaletown. Shoe guru John Fluevog (see page 65) is a son of Vancouver. Molo Design, Martha Sturdy homeware, Bocci lighting and modern woodworker Brent Comber, all darlings of the global contemporary design community, are based in the city. There is a significant movement afoot among Vancouver designers to create the eco-conscious, sustainable products that are increasingly in demand among West Coast consumers.

◆ *Go to Lululemon for your activewear*

LULULEMON

This alliterative brand name refers to a Vancouver-founded line of yoga and activewear that has developed a cult-like following across the US and beyond and spawned a host of imitators, including its own spin-off organic clothing line, Oqoqo. Every woman in Vancouver must own a pair of its comfortable, flattering, flared-leg yoga pants. At around $80 a pair the pants aren't cheap, so you might want to head to the **Lululemon factory outlet** (🄰 296 Fashion Way ☎ 360-707-2982 🖊 http://lululemon.com) in Burlington, Washington, which has reduced prices.

International designer brand outlets cluster around the Alberni Street glitter gulch and the Granville Street strip south of the bridge is home décor central. Fans of all things local and handmade will revel in poking around the Portobello West Market (see page 96). Local, independent fashion retailers are to be found in Gastown, while the area around Main Street and West 4th Avenue has a selection of boutiques offering gently-worn designer clothes. For vintage and resale furniture, Main Street is your best bet.

During the summer months, various neighbourhoods and shopping districts stage 'sidewalk sales', consisting of tables laden with bargain merchandise dotted along streets closed to all but pedestrian traffic.

Boxing Day (26 December) remains a major Canadian shopping tradition, when many stores slash prices by as much as 50 per cent.

Eating & drinking

Vancouver has been named one of the world's best restaurant cities by New York-based *Food and Wine* magazine. These days, the foodie scene is relentlessly focused on cuisine that is fresh, local and seasonal, prepared in French-influenced West Coast style. Because of the significant local Asian population, terrific Chinese, Japanese, Korean, Taiwanese, Thai, Malaysian and Vietnamese restaurants are abundant, with these exotic flavours infusing mainstream dining as well.

Foodie central is Granville Island Public Market (see page 80). In the same neighbourhood, stroll a couple of blocks west on 2nd Avenue, where you'll find a gourmet strip with the city's best cookbook store, **Barbara-Jo's Books to Cooks** (📍 1740 W 2nd Ave ☎ 604-688-6755 🌐 www.bookstocooks.com 🕐 09.00–18.00 Mon–Fri, 10.00–17.00 Sat & Sun), best cheese shop, **Les Amis du Fromage** (📍 1752 W 2nd Ave ☎ 604-732-4218 🌐 www.buycheese.com 🕐 09.00–18.00 Mon–Wed & Sat, 09.00–18.30 Thur & Fri, 09.00–17.00 Sun) and best Belgian waffles and croissants, at **Patisserie Lebeau** (📍 1728 W 2nd Ave ☎ 604-731-3528 🌐 www.grababetterwaffle.com 🕐 07.30–16.00

PRICE CATEGORIES
The restaurant price guides in this book indicate the approximate cost of a main course, not including drinks, tax or tip.

£ up to $10 ££ $10–25 £££ $25–50 £££+ over $50

⬥ *Vancouver has many fine restaurants and a wide choice of styles*

EATING GREEN

There are few places in the world with Vancouver's fervour for local, fresh, sustainably produced food. Local writers Alisa Smith and James MacKinnon tapped into the trend when they blogged about their experiment in eating locally for a year; so popular was their project, dubbed the **100-Mile Diet** (ⓦ www.100milediet.org), it spawned an eponymous book and TV show and even inspired a 100-Mile menu at local restaurant Raincity Grill (see page 70). Check local menus for the logos of **Ocean Wise** (ⓦ www.vanaqua.org/oceanwise), a group based at the Vancouver Aquarium that certifies species of edible fish for their sustainable fishing practices worldwide, and **Green Table** (ⓦ www.greentable.net), an association of local restaurateurs who meet certain standards for green business practices.

Tues–Sat). One block south is **Quince** (ⓐ 1780 W 3rd Ave ⓣ 604-731-4645 ⓦ www.quince.ca ⓛ 08.30–18.00 Mon–Sat), a cooking school, gourmet grocery and bakery.

No matter where in the city you are, there are markets packed with fresh, delicious meal and snack options (check ⓦ http://eatlocal.org for seasonal markets). Family-owned **Meinhardt** (ⓐ 3002 Granville St ⓣ 604-732-4405 ⓦ www.feedyourcuriosity.com ⓛ 09.00–19.00 Mon–Sat, 09.00–19.00 Sun) has an astonishing deli counter. The **Whole Foods Market** (ⓐ 510 W 8th Ave ⓣ 778-370-4210 ⓦ www.wholefoodsmarket.com ⓛ 08.00–22.00), is the source for all things organic and healthy.

To leave Vancouver without eating seafood would be a crime against gastronomy. Take the Aquabus from Granville Island to the Hornby dock for perennial favourite **C Restaurant** (ⓐ 1600 Howe St ❶ 604-681-1164 ⓦ www.crestaurant.com ⏰ 11.30–14.30, 17.00–late Mon–Fri, 17.00–late Sat & Sun). In Yaletown, the Blue Water Café (see page 70) serves excellent fish, shellfish and 'unsung heroes' of the sea, as well as boasting a full sushi bar. For more of a party atmosphere, try the lively **Coast Restaurant** (ⓐ 1054 Alberni St ❶ 604-685-5010 ⓦ www.coastrestaurant.ca ⏰ 11.00–00.00 Mon–Fri, 16.00–00.00 Sat & Sun). In Stanley Park, the **Fish House** (ⓐ 8901 Stanley Park Drive ❶ 604-681-7275 ⓦ www.fishhousestanleypark.com ⏰ 11.30–00.00 Ⓝ Bus: 19), is located in a rambling old heritage building. Sushi temple Tojo's (see page 88) is the place for a full *omakase* dining experience.

Note that menu prices don't include a standard tax of 5 per cent on food and 10 per cent on alcohol. Nor do they include service: in sit-down restaurants, a tip of 15–20 per cent is expected. Credit cards are accepted virtually everywhere except in farmers' markets. Smoking is not allowed in or around bars or restaurants, apart from in designated outdoor areas.

Most wine menus in local restaurants proudly list bottles from the Okanagan Valley in the interior of British Columbia, which are good value and go well with nearly all types of food. Though initially known for its heavy Cabernet Sauvignons, in recent years the Okanagan Valley has been turning out modern-style cold-climate white wines that are worth a taste. Look out for Riesling and Viognier in particular.

Entertainment & nightlife

In the early 20th century, Vancouver's still-young Downtown was lit up at dusk by the glow of neon signs, many of them marking the row of vaudeville stages and music halls along Granville Street. Now dubbed the Entertainment District, this nightlife corridor still thrives with dance clubs housed in vintage buildings, including the popular nightclub **Tonic** (ⓐ 919 Granville St ⓣ 604-669-0469 ⓦ www.thetonicclub.com ⓛ 21.00–02.00 Wed & Thur, 21.00–03.00 Fri & Sat). Also maintaining their heritage-building character are live music venues **Commodore Ballroom** (ⓐ 868 Granville St ⓣ 604-683-9413) and 19th-century bunkhouse-turned-blues club **Yale** (ⓐ 1300 Granville St ⓣ 604-681-9253 ⓦ www.theyale.ca ⓛ 12.30–02.00 Sun–Thur, 12.30–03.00 Fri & Sat).

Beware (or be tempted): the Granville Street scene is young, raucous and boozy. Note that many local cab drivers know better than to stop for obviously inebriated passengers along this route, particularly late at night, so you will want to walk over to Seymour (if northbound) or Howe (if southbound) for your best chance at a taxi. Always bring picture identification to clubs, and note that many dress codes prohibit certain clothing that bears brands or logos considered to be affiliated with gang wear.

Modern mixology has shaken and stirred the Vancouver cocktail scene, and some of the best spots for a sophisticated night of tippling include **George Ultra Lounge** (ⓐ 1127 Hamilton St ⓣ 604-628-5555 ⓦ www.georgelounge.com ⓛ 16.00–01.00 Mon–Sat ⓐ SkyTrain: Yaletown-Roundhouse), **Uva Wine Bar** (ⓐ 900 Seymour St ⓣ 604-632-9560 ⓦ www.uvawinebar.ca

🔺 *There are plenty of pubs and bars for evening entertainment*

🕐 17.00–02.00 Mon–Sat, 17.00–00.00 Sun 🚍 Bus: 4, 7, 10, 16, 17, 50) and the **Diamond** (🏠 6 Powell St 🌐 www.di6mond.com 🕐 17.30–00.00 Wed–Sun 🚍 Bus: 4, 7).

If you want to eat out as well as drink up, Vancouver's hip gastro-pubs provide a fun and inexpensive evening, with hearty but delicious food and unusual beers. A handful of options are clustered in Gastown, including the **Greedy Pig** (🏠 307 Cordova St 📞 604-669-4991 🌐 www.thegreedypig.ca 🕐 12.00–16.00 Mon, 12.00–22.00 Tues & Wed, 12.00–00.00 Thur & Fri, 14.00–00.00 Sat 🚍 Bus: 3, 4, 7, 8), **Six Acres** (🏠 203 Carrall St 📞 604-488-0110 🌐 www.sixacres.ca 🕐 17.00–01.00 Mon–Sat 🚍 Bus: 3, 4, 7, 8) and the **Irish Heather** (🏠 210 Carrall St 📞 604-688-9779 🌐 www.irishheather.com 🕐 11.30–23.00 Mon–Thur, 11.30–00.30 Fri & Sat, 12.00–00.30 Sun 🚍 Bus: 3, 4, 7, 8).

Sport & relaxation

SPECTATOR SPORTS

Team sports abound in Vancouver, and opportunities for watching matches are plentiful. For baseball fans, the minor league **Vancouver Canadians** (ⓦ www.minorleaguebaseball.com) play at the East Side Nat Bailey Stadium from June to September. July through to November is football season, with the Canadian Football League **BC Lions** (ⓦ www.bcplace.com) playing a larger-field, faster-paced version of American football at BC Place. What the Brits call football, the Canadians call soccer, and you can cheer on the **Vancouver Whitecaps** (ⓦ www.whitecapsfc.com) at the natural-turf Swangard Stadium in Burnaby between April to September. Last but not least, especially if you visit in the winter, is hockey. The Canadians love their hockey, and the National Hockey League **Vancouver Canucks** (ⓦ http://canucks.nhl.com) are always a hot ticket during the season, roughly October to April.

PARTICIPATION SPORTS
Hiking
The local litmus test for fitness is the Grouse Grind, a 3 km (1.9 mile) hike up Grouse Mountain in North Vancouver. It takes at least an hour, then there's a blissful tram ride (with a small $5 charge) down. ⓐ 6400 Nancy Greene Way, North Vancouver ⓦ www.grousemountain.com ⓝ Bus: 232, 236

Running & rollerblading
Stanley Park (see page 12) is a favourite place to jog, bike, rollerblade, walk and hike. You can actually follow the seawall

path that starts in the park all the way across Burrard Bridge either to Vanier Park and Kitsilano Park to the west, or False Creek and Yaletown (via the Cambie Bridge) to the east.

Skating

A legacy of the 2010 Olympic Winter Games is the stunning **Richmond Oval** (ⓐ 6111 River Rd, Richmond ❶ 778-296-1400 Ⓦ www.richmondoval.ca. Admission charge), where public skating and speed-skating are available along with lessons. The huge wooden roof is a modern architectural wonder and worth the trip just to see.

RELAXATION

Locals all have their favourite beaches. The most central are **English Bay** (ⓐ Beach Ave, b/n Gilford & Bidwell Sts) in Downtown's West End and **Kitsilano** (ⓐ Arbutus St & Cornwall Ave) on the south shore. The aptly named **Sunset** (ⓐ Beach Ave, b/n Thurlow & Bute Sts) is the best place to take in views of the sun falling dramatically behind the North Shore mountains. Two of the West Side beaches, **Locarno** (ⓐ NW Marine Drive, b/n Discovery & Tolmie Sts) and **Spanish Bank West** (ⓐ NW Marine Drive, west of Tolmie St) are dedicated quiet beaches, where loud music is prohibited. Beach volleyball, windsurfing and swimming are all popular.

Pets, open fires and alcohol are not permitted on public beaches. Those balking at the restrictions flock to **Wreck Beach** (ⓐ Access via Trail 6, NW Marine Drive), an 8 km (5 mile) stretch of sand on the University of British Columbia campus. Fires are still illegal here, but nudity is permitted and vendors sell alcohol, tasty food, crafts and other merchandise.

Accommodation

Accommodation is plentiful in Vancouver and there are options to suit all budgets and tastes. The tourist board website, Ⓦ www.tourismvancouver.com, has a comprehensive, searchable list of hotels, motels, apartments and hostels and can advise on good value 'room only' and package deals. Note that breakfast is not always included in the room rate.

HOTELS

Moda Hotel £ An early 20th-century building, recently renovated to include a chic wine bar, Uva, and great Italian restaurant, Cibo. The area, bordering Downtown's Granville Street club zone, can be noisy, so ask for a room that doesn't face Seymour. ⓐ 900 Seymour St (Downtown) ① 604-683-4251 Ⓦ www.modahotel.ca Ⓝ Bus: 4, 6, 10, 16, 17, 50

Sylvia Hotel £ This 1912 former apartment building has rooms and suites with kitchens and a great location near Stanley Park. Known for its Sunday brunch. ⓐ 1154 Gilford St (Downtown) ① 604-681-9321 Ⓦ www.sylviahotel.com Ⓝ Bus: 5, 6

PRICE CATEGORIES

The ratings below (unrelated to the official star system) indicate the approximate cost of a room for two people for one night, not including breakfast or tax:

£ up to $175 ££ $175–250 £££ over $250

◆ The ivy-clad Sylvia Hotel

● *Even a standard room at the Opus Hotel is quite plush*

Century Plaza Hotel & Spa ££ A family-run hotel with large, comfortable rooms, which has a Yuk Yuk's comedy club on site. Its Absolute Spa and swimming pool are big draws. ⓐ 1015 Burrard St (Downtown) ⓣ 604-687-0575 ⓦ www.century-plaza.com ⓝ Bus: 2, 22

Granville Island Hotel ££ An unbeatable location, right on Granville Island near the Public Market. Access to water taxis is easy, and though no buses go onto Granville Island itself, they do stop just outside the entrance, a five-minute walk from the hotel. ⓐ 1253 Johnson St (West Side) ⓣ 604-683-7373 ⓦ www.granvilleislandhotel.com ⓝ Bus: 50

L'Hermitage ££ This bijou design hotel in a busy Downtown shopping area is gorgeously decorated and has the advantage of boasting a pool and gym. Weekly rates offer great value. ⓐ 788 Richards St (Downtown) ⓣ 778-327-4100 ⓦ www.lhermitagevancouver.com ⓝ Bus: 5, 15

Listel Hotel ££ A self-styled art hotel, museum and gallery, displaying original works from the Museum of Anthropology and the Buschlen Mowall Art Gallery. Well located for both Downtown and the West End. ⓐ 1300 Robson St (Downtown) ⓣ 604-663-5491 ⓦ www.thelistelhotel.com ⓝ Bus: 5

Metropolitan Hotel ££ Renowned for its restaurant, Diva, this Downtown hotel often features good-value specials and packages. ⓐ 645 Howe St (Downtown) ⓣ 604-687-1122 ⓦ www.metropolitan.com ⓝ SkyTrain: Granville; bus: 4, 6, 7, 10, 16, 17, 50

Pacific Palisades ££ Part of the American Kimpton chain of budget boutique hotels, the Palisades offers complimentary wine tasting for guests nightly in the hotel art gallery. @ 1277 Robson St (Downtown) ❶ 604-688-0461 Ⓦ www.pacificpalisadeshotel.com Ⓝ Bus: 5

Plaza 500 Hotel ££ One of only a few hotels not on the Downtown side of the city, this location is convenient for South Granville shopping. The adjacent FigMint is a sleek bar and restaurant. @ 500 W 12th Ave (West Side) ❶ 604-873-1811 Ⓦ www.plaza500.com Ⓝ SkyTrain: Broadway

Loden Hotel £££ Kor Hotels, which operates several chic Los Angeles hotels, chose Vancouver for its first Canadian location. @ 1177 Melville St (Downtown) ❶ 604-669-5060 Ⓦ www.lodenvancouver.com Ⓝ Bus: 2, 19

Opus Hotel £££ A modern design-conscious hotel in Yaletown with an intimate, open lobby bar and a cosy French restaurant. Rooms are small but well appointed, with fabulous bathrooms. @ 350 Davie St (Downtown) ❶ 604-642-6787 Ⓦ www.opushotel.com Ⓝ SkyTrain: Yaletown-Roundhouse

Shangri-La £££ The first North American outpost of this luxurious Hong Kong-based hotel chain features one of only a handful of its signature Chi Spas around the world, plus the Jean-Georges Vonderichten restaurant, Market, and a swanky piano bar. @ 1128 W Georgia St (Downtown) ❶ 604-689-1120 Ⓦ www.shangri-la.com Ⓝ SkyTrain: Burrard; bus: 2, 22, 44

APARTMENTS

Cascadia Hotel & Suites ££ Full kitchens, a pool and complimentary breakfast make this Downtown hotel a good option for longer stays. 1234 Hornby St (Downtown) 604-688-1234 www.cascadiahotelvancouver.com Bus: 6

Executive Hotel Vintage Park ££ Both short-stay hotel rooms and long-stay furnished apartments are available here. Close to False Creek/Granville Island ferries and walking distance from both Downtown and Yaletown. 1379 Howe St (Downtown) 604-688-7678 www.executivehotels.net Bus: C21

Meridian at 910 Beach ££ Right on False Creek, offering suites equipped with kitchens and an in-room laundry. 910 Beach Ave (Downtown) 604-609-5100 www.910beach.com Bus: C21

HOSTELS

Hostelling International Vancouver Central £ Of Hostelling International's three Vancouver locations, this one gets the nod for having free breakfast and wireless internet. 1025 Granville St (Downtown) 604-685-5335 www.hihostels.com Bus: 4, 7, 10, 16, 17, 50

Samesun Backpacker Lodge £ Potentially noisy because of its location in Downtown's Entertainment District, but popular for its spacious communal kitchen, living room and lively Beaver Restaurant and Lounge. 1018 Granville St (Downtown) 604-682-8226 http://samesun.com SkyTrain: Granville

THE BEST OF VANCOUVER

Ocean, mountains, city: Vancouver's top sights provide a mix of urban and natural experiences that define this cosmopolitan but outdoorsy metropolis.

TOP 10 ATTRACTIONS

- **Beaches** Even in the winter, no visit to Vancouver is complete without dipping your toe in the Pacific Ocean. The city's beaches offer sunset views all year round (see page 31)

- **Stanley Park** Whether you drive, walk, run, rollerblade or bus your way through this massive urban oasis, you must experience the beating green heart of Vancouver's passion for the outdoors (see page 12)

- **Granville Island** Not only is the Public Market a foodie paradise, there are artists' studios, shops and, in a unique slice of West Coast life, a pod of float homes too (see page 80)

- **Boat trips** Not only the cute little passenger and bicycle ferries that cross False Creek but also the public SeaBus between Downtown and the North Shore are a quintessential Vancouver means of passage (see pages 56 & 74)

⬇ *Downtown Vancouver with False Creek in the foreground*

The West End Stroll this district for a peek at one of Canada's densest, liveliest and most diverse neighbourhoods (see page 58)

Robson Square A thoughtfully designed, beautifully landscaped public space, this civic square anchors Downtown and is considered an architectural master stroke (see page 18)

Museum of Anthropology Discover the heritage of the First Nations tribes that once lived here, from totem poles to longhouses (see page 82)

Vancouver Art Gallery Discover the works of Canadian artist Emily Carr, among many others, in this cutting-edge museum (see page 64)

Dining out From seafood and sushi to eco-friendly menus and farmers' markets, Vancouver is rightly known as the gourmet capital of Canada (see page 24)

Revolving restaurant A kitsch vestige of the 1960s, Vancouver's Empire Landmark hotel has a tower-top dining room which revolves as you eat. A fun and leisurely way to watch the cityscape scroll by (see page 42)

Suggested itineraries

HALF-DAY: VANCOUVER IN A HURRY

Head straight to Granville Island (see page 80), the heart of
Vancouver's foodie scene – from fresh seafood to fish and chips,
food stalls to wine boutiques and a full market. End up by browsing
artists' studios, doing a brewery tour, or going sake tasting.

1 DAY: TIME TO SEE A LITTLE MORE

When you've had your fill of Granville Island, explore Downtown
shopping, from the glittering designer stores of Alberni Street
to the hipster boutiques of Gastown. Grab a Japa Dog from a
Burrard Street cart as fuel for exploring the Vancouver Art Gallery
(see page 64). The Downtown waterfront has striking views of the
mountains to the north; to the south is the hip neighbourhood
of Yaletown, a great place to wind up the evening.

2–3 DAYS: TIME TO SEE MUCH MORE

Begin at least one day with a stroll through Stanley Park (see
page 12), or go there for a picnic. Spend a few hours exploring
the quirky shops, ethnic restaurants and elegant old heritage
buildings in the West End. Stay up for a night on the town,
trawling Granville Street's lively clubs and bars.

LONGER: ENJOYING VANCOUVER TO THE FULL

You'll have more time to discover less visited areas such as
Commercial Drive, Main Street, South Granville and Kitsilano
(see pages 78 & 90). Head to the University of British Columbia,
where the Museum of Anthropology (see page 82), Pacific Spirit

Regional Park and counter-culture Wreck Beach make fun stops. Take a day or two to explore further afield, perhaps in British Columbia's capital city Victoria (see page 116), or in the mountain town of Whistler (see page 104).

◆ Buildings at the University of British Columbia

Something for nothing

Pounding the sidewalks is always free, but information can be priceless. A free **Gastown tour** (ⓐ Gassy Jack statue, Water & Carrall Sts ⓣ 604-683-5650 ⓒ 14.00 June–Aug), chronicles the colourful characters and events of the city's oldest quarter. Or download an audio walking tour of Gastown, Chinatown, Downtown or Granville Island from **Geogad Mobile** (ⓦ www.geogad.com) – the versions with ads are free.

Although there's a small admission charge for the **Vancouver Lookout** (ⓐ 555 W Hastings St ⓣ 604-689-0421 ⓦ www.vancouverlookout.com ⓛ 08.30–22.30 May–mid-Oct; 09.00–21.00 mid-Oct–Apr ⓝ SkyTrain: Waterfront. Admission charge) on top of the towering Harbour Centre, it's definitely worth it for the view. Alternatively, you can get a similar bird's-eye view of the city for the cost of a drink or snack in Vancouver's best revolving roof-top restaurant, Cloud 9 at the Empire Landmark hotel (see page 67).

On a cultural note, the Vancouver Art Gallery (see page 64) offers admission by optional donation on Thursdays after 17.00 in low season (October to April). Jazz Vespers performances at **St Andrews Wesley United Church** (ⓐ 1022 Nelson St ⓣ 604-683-4574 ⓦ www.standrewswesleychurch.bc.ca ⓝ Bus: 2, 22, 32, 44) are free every Sunday at 16.00. **Art Starts** (ⓐ 808 Richards St ⓣ 604-878-7144 ⓦ www.artstarts.com ⓛ 10.00–17.00 ⓝ Bus: 5, 6, 20) runs free, family-oriented workshops and performances on the last Saturday of every month, ranging from clowning to drumming to dancing. For listings of more free performances, check the weekly *Georgia Straight* and *Westender* newspapers – they're also free, thankfully, and found in pick-up boxes on most streets.

To see how the other half lives, check local newspapers for real estate open houses – in a city where small flats cost half a million dollars and starter homes begin at a million, real estate is both a competitive and spectator sport.

And of course, trawling Granville Island (see page 80) for free sample titbits on the counters of butchers, bakers, cheesemongers and greengrocers is a fun – and filling – way to graze the Public Market.

The Steam Clock is just one of the interesting historical sights in Gastown

When it rains

When in Stanley Park during a rainstorm, head for the **Vancouver Aquarium** (ⓐ 845 Avison Way ⓘ 604-659-3521 ⓦ www.visitvanaqua.org ⓛ 09.30–19.00 ⓝ Bus: 19. Admission charge), home to 70,000 species, from beluga whales to sea otters. Or duck into the Fish House (see page 27) for afternoon tea.

Vanier Park in Kitsilano has three adjacent museums for an afternoon under cover: the **Vancouver Museum** (ⓐ 1100 Chestnut St ⓘ 604-736-4431 ⓦ www.museumofvancouver.ca ⓛ 10.00–17.00 Tues, Wed & Fri–Sun, 10.00–21.00 Thur ⓝ Bus: 2, 22, 32, 44. Admission charge), with fun exhibits on civic history; the **Maritime Museum** (ⓐ 1905 Ogden Ave ⓘ 604-257-8300 ⓦ www.vancouvermaritimemuseum.com ⓛ 10.00–17.00 ⓝ Bus: 2, 22, 32, 44. Admission charge), with a c. 1944 Royal Canadian Mounted Police boat you can explore; and the **HR MacMillan Space Centre** (ⓐ 1100 Chestnut St ⓘ 604-738-7827 ⓦ www.hrmacmillanspacecentre.com ⓛ 10.00–17.00 Mon–Fri, 10.00–17.00, 19.00–23.30 Sat & Sun ⓝ Bus: 2, 22, 32, 44. Admission charge), which has hourly shows and, on weekend nights, a laser light show.

Vancouver is a Pacific Rim city, so park yourself at a table at any dim sum restaurant in Chinatown, and within minutes you'll be choosing from a procession of steaming dishes that will warm any chilly day. Or get hot-stone massaged, steamed or wrapped at **Chi at Shangri-La** (ⓐ 1128 W Georgia St ⓘ 604-695-2447 ⓦ www.shangri-la.com), a unique experience in traditional Chinese healing. Located inside the luxury hotel Shangri-La, it's one of only a few Chi spas worldwide. Best for facials (for both

men and women – this is the 21st century after all) is local chain
Skoah (ⓐ 1011 Hamilton St ⓣ 604-642-0200 ⓦ www.skoah.com
ⓝ SkyTrain: Yaletown-Roundhouse).

And if you have kids in tow, you can't beat a couple of quiet hours
at the cinema on a rainy evening. As well as the ordinary movie
theatres (see page 89), try the Canada Place cruise ship terminal,
where an **IMAX Theatre** (ⓐ 999 Canada Place ⓣ 604-682-2384
ⓦ www.imax.com) offers larger-than-life entertainment.

🔺 Take a peek in the Maritime Museum at Kitsilano Beach on a rainy day

On arrival

TIME DIFFERENCE

Vancouver follows Pacific Standard Time (PST), which is eight hours behind Greenwich Mean Time (GMT). During Daylight Saving Time (mid-March to early November), clocks are put ahead by one hour.

ARRIVING

By air

The main air gateway to Vancouver is **YVR** (ⓐ 3211 Grant McConachie Way, Richmond ⓣ 604-207-7077 ⓦ www.yvr.ca Ⓝ SkyTrain: YVR-Airport), about 12 km (7½ miles) south of the city. Domestic, US and International areas of the terminal all have car rental, currency exchange and ATM services.

The new Canada Line of the **SkyTrain** (ⓦ www.translink.bc.ca) goes from the airport to Downtown Vancouver in 25 minutes for around $7.50. Alternatively, the **Airporter** shuttle bus (ⓣ 604-946-8866 ⓦ www.yvrairporter.com) leaves every 30 minutes and stops at major Downtown hotels and the Canada Place cruise ship terminal; single adults tickets cost around $14 and can be purchased on the bus or at ticket counters in the arrivals hall. You can also catch bus no. 424 from Level 1 of the Domestic Terminal to Airport Station, which allows you to connect with various useful bus routes: no. 620 goes to Tsawwassen ferry terminal, no. 100 serves Downtown Vancouver, no. 301 travels to Surrey and no. C92 is for the South Terminal. Schedules are available at Customer Service and Visitor Information counters in the arrivals hall. A single fare is approximately $2.50 (exact cash

Lions Gate Bridge, with Grouse Mountain in the background

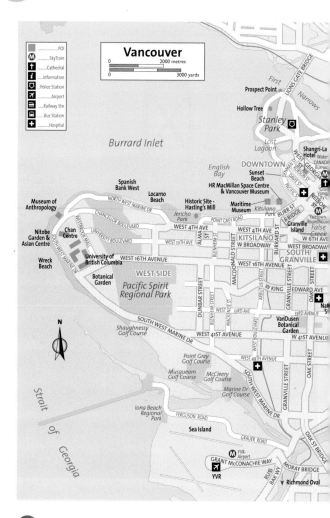

Vancouver

0	2000 metres	
0	3000 yards	

POI
SkyTrain
Cathedral
Information
Police Station
Airport
Railway Stn
Bus Station
Hospital

Burrard Inlet

First Narrows

LIONS GATE BRIDGE

Prospect Point

Hollow Tree

Stanley Park

Lost Lagoon

Shangri-La Hotel

DOWNTOWN

English Bay

Sunset Beach

HR MacMillan Space Centre & Vancouver Museum

Spanish Bank West

Locarno Beach

Historic Site - Hastings Mill

Maritime Museum

Kitsilano Park

Museum of Anthropology

Jericho Park

POINT GREY ROAD

WEST 4TH AVE

Granville Island

False Creek

NORTH WEST MARINE DR

CHANCELLOR BOULEVARD

Chan Centre

UNIVERSITY BOULEVARD

WEST 4TH AVE

W BROADWAY

KITSILANO

WEST BROADWAY

SOUTH GRANVILLE

Nitobe Garden & Asian Centre

WEST 10TH AVE

ALMA ST

BLENHEIM ST

MACDONALD STREET

BURRARD ST BRIDGE

Wreck Beach

University of British Columbia

WEST 16TH AVENUE

WEST 16TH AVENUE

ARBUTUS STREET

GRANVILLE STREET

OAK STREET

SOUTH WEST MARINE DR

WEST SIDE

Botanical Garden

Pacific Spirit Regional Park

W KING

EDWARD

VanDusen Botanical Garden

DUNBAR STREET

BLENHEIM STREET

MACKENZIE

WEST 33RD AVE

33RD AVENUE

Shaughnessy Golf Course

SOUTH WEST MARINE DR

WEST 41ST AVENUE

WEST BOULEVARD

W 41ST AVENUE

Point Grey Golf Course

WEST 49TH AVENUE

Musqueam Golf Course

McCleery Golf Course

SOUTH WEST MARINE DR

Marine Dr Golf Course

GRANVILLE STREET

OAK STREET

Iona Beach Regional Park

FERGUSON ROAD

GRAUER ROAD

OAK ST BRIDGE

Sea Island

MORAY BRIDGE

Strait of Georgia

YVR-Airport

GRANT McCONACHIE WAY

YVR

Richmond Oval

N

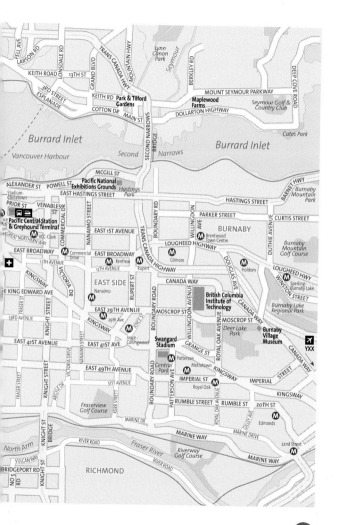

amount required), or books of Fare Saver bus tickets are available at 7-Eleven and Pharmasave stores in the domestic terminal.

If you're heading straight to Whistler (see page 104), the **SkyLynx** shuttle (☎ 604-662-7575 Ⓦ www.pacificcoach.com) runs directly from the airport to the resort, departing every couple of hours and costing approximately $50 per adult for the three-hour trip.

Taxis wait in designated areas outside each terminal's arrivals hall area. The trip to Downtown takes about 25 minutes and will cost around $30 plus a tip. Some hotels have their own complimentary shuttles.

A less common entry point is Abbotsford International Airport or **YXX** (📍 30440 Liberator Ave, Abbotsford ☎ 604-855-1001 Ⓦ www.abbotsfordairport.ca), a hub for the Western Canadian airline WestJet. As it's about 70 km (43 miles) or a one-hour drive east of Vancouver, it's convenient only if you're visiting the Fraser Valley or the suburbs. The **Valley Airporter** (☎ 604-857-7171 Ⓦ www.tourismabbotsford.ca) will take you to any address and can be reserved in advance. **Airport Link Shuttle** (☎ 604-594-3333 Ⓦ www.airportlinkshuttle.com) goes between YXX, the Canada Place cruise ship terminal, Downtown, and YVR; call for reservations and a fare quote. Taxis wait at the terminal, and you can hire one for the short ride to the nearest **Fraser Valley Transit** (☎ 604-854-3232 Ⓦ www.busonline.ca) stop or Downtown Abbotsford **Greyhound** (☎ 604-853-1691 Ⓦ www.greyhound.ca) station, where buses to Whistler, Vancouver and other points in the Lower Mainland are available. Alternatively, you can simply rent a car from one of the offices in the arrivals hall.

BUS TOURS

Since most of Vancouver's major sites are in a fairly condensed area, a hop-on, hop-off bus tour is both a useful and enjoyable way to get around. The **Vancouver Trolley Company** (☎ 888-451-5581 ⓦ www.vancouvertrolley.com) uses replica turn-of-the-century buses and costs around $35 for an adult ticket, with 24 stops en route. The **Big Bus** (☎ 604-684-5605 ⓦ www.bigbus.ca) operates bright red double-decker style buses on a 22-stop tour costing $37 per adult.

By rail

VIA Rail operates more than 450 stations across Canada, including **Pacific Central Station** (☎ 1150 Station St ☎ 888-842-7245 ⓦ www.viarail.ca) on the East Side. The station is convenient for SkyTrain's Science World-Main Street station, which can zip you into Downtown Vancouver in a few minutes. **Amtrak** (ⓦ www.amtrak.com) trains from American stations in the Pacific Northwest also arrive and depart from here.

By road

Vancouver is a well-signed, orderly and easy city in which to drive, but because of its water-bound location and many bridges, traffic can be slow. Many areas of Downtown, especially the West End, have one-way traffic restrictions. A few areas, including the busy Stanley Park Causeway leading to the Lions Gate Bridge and the North Shore, use overhead lane control signage to change traffic

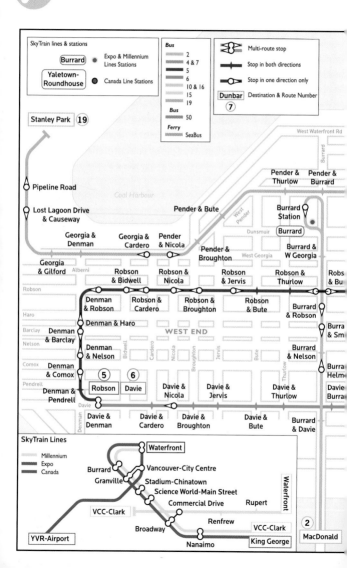

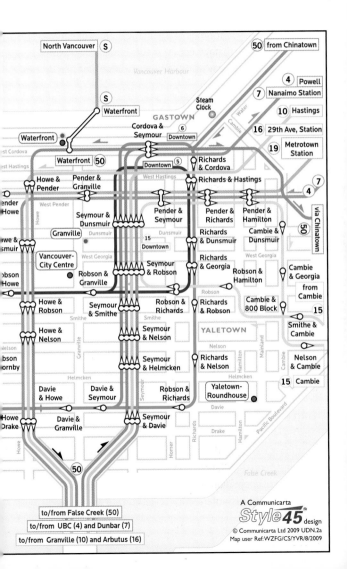

North Vancouver (S)

50 from Chinatown

4 Powell

7 Nanaimo Station

10 Hastings

(S)

Steam
Clock

16 29th Ave, Station

Waterfront

GASTOWN

19 Metrotown
Station

Waterfront

Cordova &
Seymour

6 Downtown

Waterfront 50

Downtown 5

Richards
& Cordova

West Cordova

West Hastings

Richards & Hastings

7

Howe &
Pender

Pender &
Granville

West Pender

Pender &
Seymour

Pender &
Richards

Pender &
Hamilton

4

via Chinatown

ender
Howe

Howe

Seymour &
Dunsmuir

Dunsmuir

Granville

Dunsmuir

15
Downtown

Cambie &
Dunsmuir

50

owe &
smuir

Vancouver-
City Centre

West Georgia

Richards
& Dunsmuir

Richards
& Georgia

West Georgia

Cambie
& Georgia

obson
Howe

Robson &
Granville

Seymour
& Robson

Robson

Robson &
Hamilton

from
Cambie

Howe &
Robson

Seymour
& Smithe

Smithe

Robson &
Richards

Richards
& Robson

Cambie &
800 Block

15

Howe &
Nelson

Seymour
& Nelson

Nelson

YALETOWN

Smithe &
Cambie

elson
bson
ornby

Hornby

Seymour
& Helmcken

Helmcken

Richards
& Nelson

Nelson

Helmcken

Mainland

Hamilton

Nelson
& Cambie

15 Cambie

Davie
& Howe

Davie &
Seymour

Robson &
Richards

Yaletown-
Roundhouse

Cambie

Howe
Drake

Davie &
Granville

Seymour
& Davie

Richards

Davie

Drake

Hamilton

Pacific Boulevard

50

False Creek

A Communicarta
Style 45 design
© Communicarta Ltd 2009 UDN.2a
Map user Ref:WZFG/CS/YVR/8/2009

to/from False Creek (50)

to/from UBC (4) and Dunbar (7)

to/from Granville (10) and Arbutus (16)

direction at different times of day. In most areas of Vancouver, street parking with payment at meters is inexpensive and abundant. You can pay using coins or, in some areas, credit card.

By water

Cruise ships dock at Canada Place, which also houses the Pan Pacific Hotel, shops, restaurants and places of entertainment, including an IMAX Theatre (see page 45). Day-tripping cruise passengers can store baggage at Canada Place with **CDS Baggage** (☎ 604-303-4500).

FINDING YOUR FEET

Walk, walk, walk. Most popular visitor areas of Vancouver are best seen on foot, and you'll save yourself time, money and parking hassles that way, too. Though there are relatively few SkyTrain stations, familiarise yourself with the closest bus stop to your hotel and check the sign for which routes stop there. Hotels, even if you are not a guest there, are safe and convenient places from which to catch a taxi. Vancouverites are polite and friendly and will be eager to help you with directions or information. Red-uniformed Downtown Ambassadors patrol on bike or on foot, providing hospitality assistance and security.

ORIENTATION

The five dramatic white sails of Canada Place form a handy landmark to the north, as do the North Shore mountains. The glowing neon clock faces of the vintage Vancouver Block building are a useful orientation point for the north-south spine of Granville Street and the busy intersection of Robson Street's shopping area.

Vancouver's tallest building at 61 storeys is the new Shangri-La hotel, in the heart of Downtown's business and shopping centres. If you're looking at a span of water and you see two bridges leading to mountains, you're looking at the north-facing part of Downtown and the North Shore. If you see three bridges, the vista you're looking at is south-facing Downtown, False Creek and the Lower Mainland. When confronted with a huge expanse of green and towering evergreens, chances are you are looking either at Stanley Park on the Downtown peninsula, or if you have managed to get very far-flung, Pacific Spirit Regional Park on the west tip of the Lower Mainland.

Canada Place passenger terminal by night

GETTING AROUND

Vancouver's public transit system consists of bus, SkyTrain and SeaBus routes, and is operated by **Translink** (www.translink.bc.ca), which has a handy online trip planner that provides transit instructions from your starting to end point. The SkyTrain has three lines, the latest of which, the Canada Line, opened in 2009 as the main transport link for Downtown. Buses are either electric trolleybuses or ordinary diesel vehicles.

If you plan multiple trips in a day, get a DayPass, which offers unlimited trips on the bus, SkyTrain and SeaBus for around $9. The usual single fare for a bus ride or single-zone SkyTrain trip is about $2.50. Books of ten Fare Saver tickets are available for $19, and allow a transfer within 90 minutes. Passes and tickets are widely available at 7-Eleven and Mac's convenience stores, Safeway grocery stores, London Drugs and Shopper's Drug Mart pharmacies, as well as at newsstands and corner stores. SkyTrain tickets can be purchased from self-service machines in the stations.

CAR HIRE

Car rentals are readily available at the airport, Downtown and throughout Vancouver. Members of the North America-wide car-share cooperative **Zipcar** (www.zipcar.com) can access short-term car rentals from convenient places all over Vancouver for as little as $7 an hour.

Modern curves at the Vancouver Public Library

THE CITY OF
Vancouver

Downtown

Surrounded by water, Vancouver's Downtown must be one of the most picturesque in the world. Much more than simply a business and shopping hub, it's made up of neighbourhoods with thriving residential, retail and cultural attractions of their own. Coal Harbour, to the north, is a sea of shiny condominium towers with views over the North Shore. The West End, adjacent to Stanley Park, is the densest and most diverse of Vancouver neighbourhoods, and its Davie Street spine is home to the city's gay community. Yaletown, towards the south, is a former warehouse area with a Soho-like atmosphere, filled with upscale boutiques, brick lofts and cobblestoned patios. Robson Street is Downtown's major shopping artery, defining the civic gathering place of Robson Square. Northeast of this is Gastown, the city's oldest area and today a gentrified quarter of hipster shops, restaurants and bars.

SIGHTS & ATTRACTIONS

Chinatown

The cultural home of the city's largest ethnic group is marked by an ornate Millennium Gate at Taylor and Pender Streets. Follow the street banners for a Silk Road tour of herbalist shops, the Sam Kee Building (the world's narrowest at just 1.83 m (6 ft), according to Ripley's), the **Dr. Sun Yat-Sen Classical Chinese Garden** (ⓐ 578 Carrall St ⓣ 604-662-3207 ⓦ www.vancouverchinesegarden.com ⓛ 09.00–19.00 ⓝ SkyTrain: Stadium-Chinatown; bus: 19, 22. Admission charge) and a massive bell from the Han Dynasty

◔ *A peaceful ambience at Dr. Sun Yat-Sen Classical Chinese Garden*

Downtown

		POI
Ⓜ		SkyTrain
✝		Cathedral
ⓘ		Information
☉		Police Station
✈		Airport
🚃		Railway Stn
🚌		Bus Station
✚		Hospital

0 · 500 metres
0 · 500 yards

STANLEY PARK DRIVE
Totem Poles

Hallelujah Point

DEADMAN'S ISLAND

HMCS Discovery
(Naval Training Centre)

Burrard Inlet

Vancouver Harbour

SeaBus to Lonsdale Quay, North Vancouver

IMAX Theatre &
Vancouver Convention
Centre

Harbour
Green Park

CANADA
PLACE

SeaBus Terminal

HASTINGS STREET

PENDER ST

Waterfront Ⓜ

ⓘ

Burrard Ⓜ

Bill Reid
Gallery ⑪

Vancouver
Lookout ⑤ GASTOWN

'Gassy'
Jack Deighton
Statue

Portside
Park

WATER ST
BLOOD ALLEY

⑭
⑧

WATERFRONT RD

WATERFRONT
ROAD

RAILWAY ST

RAILWAY AVE

DUNLEVY AVE

JACKSON AVE

BURRARD STREET

HOWE STREET

STREET

HASTINGS STREET

DOWNTOWN

①

Vancouver
Art Gallery

Robson
Square

Vancouver
Block

Orpheum
Theatre

HORNBY STREET

DUNSMUIR STREET

Granville/
Vancouver
City Centre

RICHARDS STREET

✝

W CORDOVA ST

ALEXANDER STREET

POWELL STREET

Victory
Square

COLUMBIA ST

CARRALL ST

Openheimer
Park

EAST CORDOVA STREET

EAST HASTINGS STREET

SEYMOUR ST

RICHARDS STREET

HOMER STREET

WEST GEORGIA STREET

HAMILTON STREET

CAMBIE STREET

PENDER STREET

⑥

KEEFER STREET

CHINATOWN

Dr Sun Yat-Sen
Classical Chinese
Garden

MAIN STREET

PENDER STREET EAST

KEEFER ST

E GEORGIA ST

UNION

CORE AVENUE

JACKSON AVENUE

STREET

GRANVILLE

SMITHE STREET

MAINLAND STREET

NELSON STREET

HOMER STREET

BEATTY STREET

Vancouver
Public Library

Stadium-
Chinatown Ⓜ

PACIFIC BLVD NORTH

DUNSMUIR VIADUCT

GEORGIA VIADUCT

PRIOR STREET

⑩

EXPO BLVD

YALETOWN

own PACIFIC BLVD
thouse

MARINSIDE CRESCENT

BC Place

Cooper's
Park

PACIFIC BLVD

Plaza of
Nations

CAMBIE BRIDGE

False Creek

Creekside
Park

Science
World
Science
World-
Main
Street Ⓜ

MAIN STREET

Thornton
Park

Pacific Central
Station

Greyhound
Terminal

in Shanghai Alley. ⓐ Bordered by Hastings, Keefer, Gore and Taylor Sts ⓦ www.vancouverchinatown.ca

Shangri-La Hotel

The tallest building in Vancouver at 61 storeys, this luxury hotel was opened in 2009 as the first North American outpost of the Hong Kong-based luxury hotel chain. It has one of only a handful of the renowned Chi spas in the world (see page 44). Even if you can't afford to stay here, you can gaze up at it from the outside or pop in to enjoy a quiet drink in the lobby's piano bar. ⓐ 1128 W Georgia St ⓣ 604-689-1120 ⓦ www.shangri-la.com ⓝ SkyTrain: Burrard

Vancouver Convention Centre

A state-of-the-art eco-friendly building, built using natural materials and boasting a waterfront location, enormous green roof and underground fish habitat, this complex is a joy to explore. Tours of the building are available in off-peak periods. ⓐ 1055 Canada Place ⓣ 604-646-3561 ⓦ www.vancouverconventioncentre.com ⓛ Tours: 10.00, 11.30, 13.30, 15.00 by reservation ⓝ SkyTrain: Waterfront

CULTURE

Bill Reid Gallery

The most celebrated artist in the First Nations Haida cultural tradition, the late Bill Reid worked extensively with precious metals as the exquisite jewellery in this bijou gallery demonstrates. Reid is well known for his massive sculptures, like Jade Canoe at YVR airport, but this gallery showcases his more intimate, small-scale

Vancouver Convention Centre

works. ⓐ 639 Hornby St ⓣ 604-682-3455 ⓦ www.billreidgallery.ca
ⓛ 11.00–17.00 Wed–Sun Ⓝ SkyTrain: Burrard or Granville

Vancouver Art Gallery

Located in a regal c. 1905 courthouse, this world-class fine art
museum has exemplar Emily Carr and Group of Seven painting
in its 9,000-work collection. The on-site Gallery Café has an
outdoor patio that makes a nice spot for a glass of wine,
a sandwich and a breather. ⓐ 750 Hornby St ⓣ 604-662-4719
ⓦ www.vanartgallery.bc.ca ⓛ 10.00–17.30 Mon, Wed & Fri–Sun,
10.00–21.00 Tues & Thur Ⓝ SkyTrain: Granville

Vancouver Public Library

Renowned Canadian architect Moshe Safdie created this coliseum-
like complex, housing 1.2 million books. The building is a venue
for frequent author readings, cultural events and book clubs.
Internet access available. ⓐ 350 W Georgia St ⓣ 604-331-3603
ⓦ www.vpl.vancouver.bc.ca ⓛ 10.00–21.00 Mon–Thur, 10.00–18.00
Fri & Sat, 10.00–17.00 Sun Ⓝ SkyTrain: Stadium-Chinatown

RETAIL THERAPY

There is something for every price range in Downtown,
from discount emporium **Army & Navy** (ⓐ 36 W Cordova St
ⓣ 604-682-6644 ⓦ www.armyandnavy.ca ⓛ 09.30–18.00
Mon–Wed & Sat, 09.30–21.00 Thur & Fri, 11.00–18.00 Sun) to
global designers. For local products and unique shops, head
to Gastown, where you'll find premium denim provider **Dutil**
(ⓐ 303 W Cordova St ⓣ 604-688-8892 ⓦ www.dutildenim.com

ART CITY

The 'Vancouver School' is a renowned contemporary movement sparked by photo-conceptual artists like Jeff Wall, Roy Arden, Stan Douglas and Rodney Graham in the 1980s. Independently of one another, these artists began producing stills, lightboxes and films featuring highly realistic images on subjects relevant to the social issues of the day. For instance, Jeff Wall's backlit lightbox *The Pine on the Corner* depicts a towering evergreen (now cut down) dwarfing modest two-storey dwellings on a wintery Vancouver street, the North Shore mountains glowering in the background: a subtle but unmistakable comment on urban infringement of the natural habitat. Today, the next wave to build upon the legacy of the Vancouver School is a generation of photo-conceptual street artists who are covering the Downtown Eastside and beyond with new-school postering and photo-tagging – a movement that's still under the radar but easy to access. Ⓦ www.flickr.com has a good gallery of Vancouver street art.

Ⓛ 11.00–19.00 Mon–Wed & Sat, 11.00–20.00 Thur & Fri, 12.00–17.00 Sun) and the flagship store of Vancouver-born shoe king **John Fluevog** (Ⓐ 65 Water St Ⓣ 604-688-2879 Ⓦ www.fluevog.com Ⓛ 11.00–19.00 Mon–Wed & Sat, 11.00–20.00 Thur & Fri, 12.00–18.00 Sun Ⓢ SkyTrain: Granville), as well as local designer showcase the **Block** (Ⓐ 350 W Cordova St Ⓣ 604-685-8885 Ⓦ www.theblock.ca Ⓛ 11.00–18.00

Mon–Thur & Sat, 11.00–19.00 Fri, 12.00–17.00 Sun). On the neighbourhood's edge, don't miss design emporium **Provide** (📍 529 Beatty St 📞 604-632-0095 🌐 www.providehome.com 🕐 11.00–18.00).

BeautyMark The Vancouver founder of Supply Cosmetics created this unique Yaletown beauty emporium which has make-up artist on site. 📍 1120 Hamilton St 📞 604-687-2294 🌐 www.beautymark.ca 🕐 10.00–19.00 Mon–Sat 🚇 SkyTrain: Yaletown-Roundhouse

Hudson's Bay Company Canada's oldest department store retailer has a massive location in a heritage building at Granville and Georgia Streets, which is the place to find modern products – from blankets and pillows to jackets – sporting the company's distinctive red, green and blue-striped heritage pattern. 📍 674 Granville St 📞 604-681-6211 🌐 www.thebay.com 🕐 09.30–19.00 Mon, Tues & Sat, 09.30–21.00 Wed–Fri, 11.00–19.00 Sun 🚇 SkyTrain: Granville

Leone Indulge in a truly Vancouver shopping experience at this family-run luxury goods emporium, which carries Dior, Prada, Armani and other international heavy hitters. The L2 boutique downstairs offers more casual styles and has a café. 📍 757 Hastings St 📞 604-683-1133 🌐 www.leone.ca 🕐 10.00–18.00 Mon–Sat, 12.00–17.00 Sun 🚇 SkyTrain: Waterfront

Taylorwood Wines In the interior of British Columbia, the Okanagan Valley wine region has been winning accolades for its cold-climate white wines and red blends. Find a selection of the province's best at this Yaletown boutique, where all the bottles carry the province's VQA mark of quality. 🄰 1185 Mainland St 🄸 604-408-9463 🔞 www.taylorwoodwines.com 🄻 10.00–21.00 Mon–Sat, 12.00–19.00 Sun 🄽 SkyTrain: Yaletown-Roundhouse

TAKING A BREAK

Downtown teems with casual dining options, including chains like Cactus Club, Joey's, Earl's and Milestones. For a drink or snack with a view, try the revolving **Cloud 9** restaurant (🄰 1400 Robson St 🄸 604-687-0511 🔞 www.cloud9restaurant.ca 🄻 Restaurant: 06.00–10.30, 17.00–22.00; lounge: 17.00–23.30 Mon–Wed, 17.00–00.00 Fri & Sat) at the Empire Landmark hotel.

Caffè Artigiano £ ❶ This local chain brought 'latte art' to the masses a decade ago and still swirls a perfect heart, leaf or other design on the foamy surface of its excellent espresso-based drinks. 🄰 763 Hornby St 🄸 604-694-7737 🔞 www.caffeartigiano.com 🄻 06.30–21.00 Mon–Fri, 07.00–21.00 Sat, 07.00–19.00 Sun 🄽 Bus: 4, 7, 10, 16, 17, 50

Fritz European Fry House £ ❷ A popular late-night haunt but good for a snack any time of the day, this fry house serves generous cones of chips with a choice of nearly two dozen dips and toppings. A popular option is the Quebec favourite *poutine*: fries topped with gravy and curd cheese. 🄰 718 Davie St 🄸 604-684-0811 🔞 www.fritzeuropeanfryhouse.com 🄻 11.30–02.30 Tues & Wed, 11.30–03.30 Thur, 11.30–04.00 Fri, 12.00–04.00 Sat, 13.00–02.30 Sun 🄽 Bus: 4, 7, 10, 16, 17, 50

○ *Caffè Artigiano is renowned for its 'latte-art' designs*

Japa Dog £ ❸ These Japanese-influenced hot dog carts specialise in delicious *kurobuta* pork wieners served in unique flavour combinations. Try 'Okonomi' – Japanese mayonnaise, fried cabbage, bonito flakes, okonimi sauce. ⓐ Burrard St; also at Smithe St and other locations, check website ⓦ www.japadog.com ⓛ 12.00–19.30 Mon–Thur, 12.00–20.00 Fri & Sat, 12.30–19.00 Sun ⓝ Bus: 2, 22

Nat's New York Pizzeria £ ❹ For fresh, hot slices of thin, hand-tossed crust pie, locals swear by this West End favourite. ⓐ 1080 Denman St ⓣ 604-642-0777 ⓦ www.natspizza.com ⓛ 11.00–22.00 Mon–Sat, 12.00–21.00 Sun ⓝ Bus: 5

So.Cial Custom Butcher Shop £ ❺ Imaginative lunchtime sandwiches are served at this Gastown artisan butcher, made with the finest charcuterie and cheese and served with homemade potato chips. ⓐ 332 Water St ⓣ 604-669-4488 ⓦ www.socialatlemagasin.com ⓛ 07.30–19.00 Mon–Sat, 12.00–18.00 Sun ⓝ Bus: 44

Medina ££ ❻ This next-door café sibling to fine-dining restaurant Chambar developed a following for its Belgian-style waffles and coffee. ⓐ 556 Beatty St ⓣ 604-879-3114 ⓦ www.medinacafe.com ⓛ 08.00–17.00 Tues–Fri, 09.00–16.00 Sat & Sun ⓝ SkyTrain: Stadium-Chinatown; bus: 50

AFTER DARK

Live music and clubs are based around the Granville Street corridor known as the Entertainment District, swanky restaurants abound in Yaletown and fun wine bars and tapas lounges are everywhere.

RESTAURANTS

Raincity Grill ££ A cosy and romantic West End restaurant with gorgeous views of English Bay. There's an excellent *Wine Spectator*-anointed wine list, and the 100-Mile tasting menu (from which all items are made from foods sourced in that local radius) remains a perennial favourite. ⓐ 1193 Denman St ⓣ 604-685-7337 ⓦ www.raincitygrill.com ⓛ 11.30–14.30, 17.00–22.30 Mon–Fri, 10.30–15.00, 17.00–22.30 Sat & Sun ⓝ Bus: 5

Boneta £££ The cool DIY décor (Dali-esque mirrors chained to the ceiling, huge canvases) is matched by a menu, projected onto the wall each night, that showcases the best local, seasonal ingredients in French-influenced preparation. ⓐ 1 W Cordova St ⓣ 604-684-1844 ⓦ www.boneta.ca ⓛ 17.30–00.00 Mon–Sat ⓝ Bus: 50

Cioppino's Mediterranean Grill £££ The best Italian cooking in Vancouver is here in Yaletown, where you might see celebrities sneaking in their carb fix. ⓐ 1133 Hamilton St ⓣ 604-688-7466 ⓦ www.cioppinos.wordpress.com ⓛ 17.30–00.00 Tues–Sat ⓝ SkyTrain: Yaletown-Roundhouse

Blue Water Café £££+ Whether it's sushi or seafood you crave, it's all here at this sophisticated Yaletown eatery. The Unsung Heroes menu features delicious, innovatively prepared tasting portions of the sea's lesser-known creatures. ⓐ 1095 Hamilton St ⓣ 604-688-8078 ⓦ www.bluewatercafe.net ⓛ 17.00–01.00 (kitchen closes 23.00) ⓝ SkyTrain: Yaletown-Roundhouse

◆ *Posh dining on the outdoor patio at Blue Water Café*

Hy's Encore £££+ ⓫ For an old-fashioned steakhouse meal you can't beat this classy, portrait-lined meat den. This is the only place in town that still charcoal-grills its steaks. ⓐ 637 Hornby ⓣ 604-683-7671 ⓦ www.hyssteakhouse.com ⓒ 11.30–15.00, 17.00–23.30 Mon–Fri, 17.00–23.30 Sat & Sun ⓝ Bus: 4, 7, 10, 16, 17, 50

WINE BARS & TAPAS LOUNGES

Bin 941 ££ ⓬ This pocket-size wine bar and tapas lounge kicked off a major small-plates dining and grazing trend when it opened a decade ago. ⓐ 941 Davie St ⓣ 604-683-1246 ⓦ www.bin941.com ⓒ 17.00–01.30 Mon–Sat, 17.00–00.00 Sun ⓝ Bus: 6

Kingyo Izakaya ££ ⓭ An *izakaya*, or Japanese gastro-pub, where you can order a tall bamboo stem of sake and taste specialities like thin slices of beef tongue grilled on a hot stone. ⓐ 871 Denman St ⓣ 604-608-1677 ⓦ www.kingyo-izakaya.com ⓒ 17.30–00.00 ⓝ Bus: 5

Salt Tasting Room ££ ⓮ An eating place without a kitchen, this sleek wine bar has a high-concept menu that involves only charcuterie and cheese with bread and condiments. ⓐ 45 Blood Alley ⓣ 604-633-1912 ⓦ www.salttastingroom.com ⓒ 12.00–00.00 ⓝ Bus: 10, 16, 20

Sanafir ££ ⓯ A sexy Middle Eastern vibe lounge with create-your-own tasting platters. Reserve one of the draped lounging beds upstairs and ask to have a bottle of chilled champagne waiting for you on arrival. ⓐ 1026 Granville St ⓣ 604-678-1049 ⓦ www.sanafir.ca ⓒ 17.00–01.00 ⓝ Bus: 4, 6, 7, 10, 16, 17, 50

BARS & CLUBS

1181 The see-and-be-seen gay (but straight-friendly) bar on the Davie Street strip has a retro-chic teak, cedar and cork interior and cocktail menu headings that might just describe your mood at the time (fresh, fruity, tart?). ⓐ 1181 Davie St ⓣ 604-687-3991 ⓦ www.tightlounge.com ⓛ 11.00–01.00 ⓝ Bus: 6

Bacchus The lounge in the elegant Wedgewood Hotel is the kind of old-school bar where fishbowl-sized martinis are poured at your table. ⓐ 845 Hornby St ⓣ 604-608-5319 ⓦ www.wedgewoodhotel.com ⓛ Until 00.00 ⓝ Bus: 4, 7, 10, 16, 17, 50

Celebrities A gay club where everyone's welcome, with nightly DJs and often international stars as guest performers. ⓐ 1022 Davie St ⓣ 604-681-6180 ⓦ www.celebritiesnightclub.com ⓛ 21.00–02.00 Tues–Thur & Sat, 21.00–03.00 Fri, 21.00–00.00 Sun ⓝ Bus: 6

George Ultra Lounge To make the cocktails at this swank Yaletown lounge, the 'bar chefs' have a cornucopia of fresh fruits and herbs on display. ⓐ 1137 Hamilton St ⓣ 604-628-5555 ⓦ www.georgelounge.com ⓛ 17.00–01.00 Mon & Tues, 17.00–02.00 Wed–Sat ⓝ SkyTrain: Yaletown-Roundhouse

Republic The most upscale of the Downtown clubs, this two-storey joint plays mostly house music, with a weekly '80s-themed ladies' night. ⓐ 958 Granville St ⓣ 604-669-3266 ⓦ www.donnellynightclubs.com ⓛ 21.00–03.00 Thur–Sat ⓝ Bus: 4, 7, 10, 16, 17, 50

West Side

Vancouver's West Side is a leafy green haven. At its most wester
end, the University of British Columbia campus owns the vast
Pacific Spirit Regional Park (www.greatervancouverparks.cor
Bus: 4, 44, 84), with over 50 km (30 miles) of forested trails fo
walking, cycling, running or picnicking. Beaches dot the northwe
coast of the Lower Mainland, with one to suit everyone from
families to nudists to canine lovers. Further than most visitors
usually venture, the wealthy neighbourhoods of Shaughnessy
and Kerrisdale are where some of the city's moneyed elite and
yuppie families reside. It's worth the trip here to stroll through
the **VanDusen Botanical Garden** (5251 Oak St 604-878-927.
www.vandusengarden.org 10.00–dusk Bus: 17. Admissio
charge) in summer, when concerts and events take place in the
park, or in winter when it twinkles with festive lights. Kitsilano,
former hippie and American draft-dodger enclave, is now a thrivin
neighbourhood for young professionals that has replaced its thri
shops and diners with sleek boutiques and trendy restaurants,
but still retains a laid-back beachside feel. The adjacent Point
Grey residential area is made up of streets lined with grand
old flowering trees and genteel vintage houses.

SIGHTS & ATTRACTIONS

False Creek cruises

The view of Vancouver from the water is magical. In warmer month
your options include evening dinner cruises (604-681-2915
www.vancouvercruises.com), but one-hour water taxi tours

◆ *Meander through the VanDusen Botanical Garden*

West Side

0 — 500 metres

0 — 500 yards

● *Popular Kitsilano Beach*

☎ 604-684-7781 Ⓦ www.granvilleislandferries.bc.ca or
☎ 604-689-5858 Ⓦ http://theaquabus.com) can be just as fun
and operate throughout the year. Call for options, times & prices.

Granville Island Brewing

Canada's first microbrewery opened in 1984 and is still going strong.
It offers a tour that ends with a tasting of samplers of all the brand's
standard (pilsner, lager, honey lager, cream ale) and exotic seasonal
beers. ⓐ 1441 Cartwright St ☎ 604-687-2739 Ⓦ www.gib.ca
🕐 Tours: 12.00, 14.00, 16.00 Ⓝ Bus: 50. Admission charge

Kitsilano Beach & Pool

A family-friendly beach and park featuring a heated saltwater pool that offers both lane swimming and recreational splashing possibilities. Massive driftwood logs are the beach's most popular perches, while the Watermark beachside café is a great spot for a bite to eat. ⓐ 2305 Cornwall Avenue ⓣ 604-731-0011 ⓦ www.vancouver.ca ⓛ 12.00–20.45 mid-May–mid-Sept ⓝ Bus: 2, 22. Admission charge for pool

Miraj Hammam Spa

One of only a handful of authentic Turkish hammams in North America, this unique day spa offers traditional steam-exfoliation

GRANVILLE ISLAND

False Creek's former industrial areas were transformed into an urban playground in the 1970s and are now one of Vancouver's most visited, and pleasant, spots. As well as containing the city's foodie central Public Market, the easily walkable parcel of waterfront land features everything from fish and chips stalls to artists' studios, street performers, and wine, sake and beer stores. It's also a taking-off point for water taxis to the Downtown side of False Creek (see page 74) and to nearby **Bowen Island** (ⓦ www.giwt.ca), plus a gateway to a pretty recreational seawall lining False Creek. A highlight is **Edible British Columbia** (ⓘ 604-662-3606 ⓦ www.edible-britishcolumbia.com ⓛ 09.00–19.00 ⓝ Bus: 50), a source for locally-made products and a clearinghouse for culinary information and resources; its culinary market tours are a perfect rainy day activity. Stop at any of the fishmongers to taste Indian Candy, snack-size sticks of smoked salmon cured in maple syrup. For more information, see ⓦ www.granvilleisland.com.

cleansing treatments. End up by relaxing on cushy day beds in the Sultana Lounge and enjoying delicious mint tea and cake. ⓐ 1495 W 6th Ave ⓣ 604-733-5151 ⓦ www.mirajhammam.com ⓛ 11.00–19.00 Tues–Thur, 12.00–20.00 Fri, 10.00–18.00 Sat ⓝ Bus: 4, 7, 10, 16, 17, 50

Vanier Park

Adjacent to Kitsilano Beach, this park is dotted with museums and attractions (see page 44) and, in the summer, hosts festivals and makes a perfect picnic spot. ⓐ 1100 Chestnut St ❶ 604-257-8400 ⓦ www.greatervancouverparks.com Ⓝ Bus: 2, 22

CULTURE

Arts Club Theatre

An adventurous slate of modern international and Canadian works make up the annual season of this theatre company, with stages on **Granville Island** (ⓐ 1585 Johnston St) and in the vintage **Stanley Theatre** (ⓐ 2750 Granville St). ❶ 604-687-1644 ⓦ www.artsclub.com Ⓝ Bus: 50 for Granville Island; bus: 10 for Stanley Theatre

Gallery Row

More than a dozen art galleries cluster around several blocks of Granville just south of the bridge, making for a full afternoon of art. For contemporary art, head to **Douglas Udell Gallery** (ⓐ 1558 W 6th Ave ❶ 604-736-8900 ⓦ www.douglasudellgallery.com), **Diane Farris Gallery** (ⓐ 1590 W 7th Ave ❶ 604-737-2629 ⓦ www.dianefarrisgallery.com), **Equinox Gallery** (ⓐ 2321 Granville St ❶ 604-736-2405 ⓦ www.equinoxgallery.com) and **Petley Jones** (ⓐ 2235 Granville St ❶ 604-732-5353 ⓦ www.petleyjones.com). Canadian and West Coast art can be found at **Heffel** (ⓐ 2247 Granville St ❶ 604-732-6505 ⓦ www.heffel.com), **Kurbatoff Gallery** (ⓐ 2427 Granville St ❶ 604-736-5444 ⓦ www.kurbatoffgallery.com) and **Douglas Reynolds Gallery** (ⓐ 2335 Granville St ❶ 604-731-9292 ⓦ http://douglasreynoldsgallery.com). For something different,

browse Asian art at **Jacana Gallery** (📍 2435 Granville St
📞 604-879-9306 🌐 www.jacanagallery.com) and **Bau-Xi**
(📍 3045 Granville St 📞 604-733-7011 🌐 www.bau-xi.com).
For more information on Gallery Row and the surrounding
area, see 🌐 www.southgranville.org.

Museum of Anthropology

A stunning museum which is as famous for its grounds
(featuring two traditional Haida longhouses and ten full-size
totem poles) as for the fascinating collection of artefacts inside,
which come from indigenous cultures around the world. The
unusual building was designed by the late architect Arthur
Erickson, based on Pacific Northwest post and beam structures.
📍 6393 NW Marine Drive 📞 604-822-5087 🌐 www.moa.ubc.ca
🕐 10.00–17.00 Wed–Sun, 10.00–21.00 Tues 🚌 Bus: 4, 44, 84

Vancouver TheatreSports League

The wacky comedy troupe performs most nights at the
New Revue Stage on Granville Island. 📍 1601 Johnston St
📞 604-738-7013 🌐 www.vtsl.com 🚌 Bus: 50

RETAIL THERAPY

Duthie's Books A 50-year-old Vancouver institution and one
of the few remaining independent bookstores in the city, this
lovely shop has local and Canadian literature as well as the broad
selection you'd expect from any major bookseller. 📍 2239 W 4th
Ave 📞 604-732-5344 🌐 www.duthiebooks.com 🕐 09.00–21.00
Mon–Fri, 09.00–18.00 Sat, 10.00–18.00 Sun 🚌 Bus: 4, 7, 84

⬥ *Monumental arch and totem in the Museum of Anthropology*

Gravity Pope A world-class selection of hip, mostly casual shoes for men and women is the hallmark of this Western Canadian retailer. Next door at no. 2203 is its equally trendy clothing boutique, Gravity Pope Tailored Goods. 🅰 2205 W 4th Ave 📞 604 731-7673 🕐 10.00–21.00 Mon–Fri, 10.00–19.00 Sat, 11.00–18.00 Sun 🅝 Bus: 4, 7, 84

Moulé A lifestyle boutique featuring an international designer range of clothing and accessories for men and women, items for the home, and toys for very cool kids. 🅰 1994 W 4th Ave 📞 604-732-4066 🅦 www.moulestores.com 🕐 10.00–18.00 Mon–Wed & Sat, 10.00–21.00 Thur–Fri, 11.00–18.00 Sun 🅝 Bus: 4, 7, 84

TAKING A BREAK

49th Parallel £ ❶ The family originally behind the Caffè Artigiano chain has opened a wicked artisanal café in Kitsilano. It's the city's best cup, whether you prefer Clover-brewed or espresso-style coffee made from its own roasts or fair trade and organic teas. Choose from a small selection of excellent baked goods, from chocolate croissants to biscotti. 🅰 2152 W 4th Ave 📞 604-420-4900 🅦 www.49thparallelroasters.com 🕐 07.00–21.00 🅝 Bus: 4, 7, 84

Noodle Box £ ❷ Stir-fried noodle dishes in pan-Asian flavours from Pad Thai to Japanese teriyaki are made to order at your desired level of spice. Dumplings, satays, curries and a small selection of beer and wine make this a great lunch or casual dinner option. 🅰 1867 W 4th Ave 📞 604-734-1310 🅦 http://thenoodlebox.net 🕐 11.30–21.00 Sat–Thur, 11.30–22.00 Fri 🅝 Bus: 4, 7, 84

Patisserie Lebeau £ ❸ Both sweet (dipped in dark or milk chocolate) and savoury (in a dozen flavours, including a killer green onion and cheese version) styles of Belgian waffles are made fresh daily here. Stop by at lunchtime for innovative waffle sandwiches (try chicken and brie) and stuffed baguettes. ❸ 1728 W 2nd Ave ❶ 604-731-3528 Ⓦ www.grababetterwaffle.com ❶ 07.30–16.00 Tues–Sat Ⓝ Bus: 50

Picnic £ ❹ The café owned by gourmet grocery Meinhardt is perfect for lunch or a restorative snack while exploring the area. ❸ 3002 Granville St ❶ 604-732-4405 Ⓦ www.meinhardt.com ❶ 07.00–19.00 Mon–Fri, 08.00–19.00 Sat, 08.00–18.00 Sun Ⓝ Bus: 10

T £ ❺ The delicately flavoured teas from this Vancouver-based company grace some of the world's finest establishments, from Jean-Georges restaurants to St Regis hotels. The flagship Vancouver tasting room and shop allows you to sample more than 100 blends and is packed with gorgeous accessories. ❸ 1568 W Broadway ❶ 604-730-8390 Ⓦ www.tealeaves.com ❶ 09.30–19.00 Mon–Sat, 11.00–18.00 Sun Ⓝ Bus: 9, 16, 17

Go Fish ££ ❻ Only in Vancouver would a fish and chips shack boast that it serves sustainably-fished seafood from local fisherman. The halibut and crispy chips are crowd pleasers, but for more refined palates, the salmon or tuna *tacones* (soft flour tortillas rolled into a cone) make a delicious snack. Follow the walking path west from Granville Island or look for signs for the fish-sales docks. ❸ 1505 W 1st Ave ❶ 604-730-5040 ❶ 11.30–18.00 Wed–Fri, 12.00–18.00 Sat & Sun Ⓝ Bus: 50

Sophie's Cosmic Café ££ ❼ A funky all-day café with the ambience of a vintage diner, this Kitsilano neighbourhood institution has memorabilia-packed walls, red vinyl booths and friendly service (kids love it here). Massive breakfasts, chunky sandwiches and hulking desserts draw queues of hungry people. ⓐ 2095 W 4th Ave ❶ 604-732-6810 Ⓦ www.sophiescosmiccafe.com Ⓛ 08.00–21.30 Ⓝ Bus: 4, 7, 84

Trafalgars ££ ❽ Infiltrate the everyday world of the locals at this Point Grey neighbourhood bistro, which has excellent gourmet brunches and surprisingly sophisticated lunch and dinner fare. Service is lovely, and desserts include feather-light, sky-high cakes and pies from the Sweet Obsession bakery next door. ⓐ 2603 W 16th Ave ❶ 604-739-0554 Ⓦ www.trafalgars.com Ⓛ 09.00–00.00 Mon–Sat, 09.00–16.00 Sun Ⓝ Bus: 33

AFTER DARK

RESTAURANTS

Fuel ££ ❾ Through this upmarket restaurant's glass storefront you can see renegade chef Robert Belcham (he has colourful tattoos down both arms) prepping in the kitchen. Try Fried Chicken Fridays for a fun lunch. At dinner co-owner and sommelier Tom Doughty might just recommend a bottle of his own vintage from the interior of British Columbia. ⓐ 1944 W 4th Ave ❶ 604-288-7905 Ⓦ www.fuelrestaurant.ca Ⓛ 11.30–14.30, 17.30–00.00 Ⓝ Bus: 4, 7, 84

Maenam ££ ❿ Offering Thai cuisine loaded with fresh herbs, hot spice and authentic flavours, this simple but elegant Kitsilano

restaurant has exotic and innovative cocktails and a well-matched list of refreshing wines. **a** 1938 W 4th Ave **t** 604-730-5579 **L** 11.30–22.00 **N** Bus: 4, 7, 84

Memphis Blues ££ ⓫ American-style barbecue – pork, beef and other meats cooked 'low and slow' in a hardwood-burning smoker – is hard to find in Vancouver, but this casual joint has nailed it. The pulled pork sandwich dressed with 'slaw is a good lunch, while the Elvis Platter serves several for dinner. Other specialities include fried catfish and wild game. Sophisticated beer and wine menu. **a** 1465 W Broadway **t** 604-738-6806 **w** www.memphisbluesbbq.com **L** 11.00–22.00 Mon–Thur, 11.00–23.00 Fri, 12.00–23.00 Sat, 12.00–22.00 Sun **N** Bus: 9

The Naam ££ ⓬ Vegetarian options or special requests are mainstream at Vancouver restaurants, but entirely vegetarian restaurants are still few. This long-time favourite – open 24/7 all year round except Christmas day – still draws queues for its Dragon Bowls and other Asian-inflected dishes. **a** 2724 W 4th Ave **t** 604-738-7151 **w** www.thenaam.com **L** 24 hrs **N** Bus: 4, 7, 84

Vij's ££ ⓭ Proprietor Vikram Vij has a worldwide following for this chic, modern Indian restaurant that somehow manages to keep its cosy atmosphere. The lamb popsicles in fenugreek curry sauce are legendary. You'll probably have to wait to be seated, but eating tiny, tasty pakoras and other snacks in the back bar and waiting room is one of the pleasures of a leisurely evening here. **a** 1480 W 11th Ave **t** 604-736-6664 **w** www.vijs.ca **L** 17.30–00.00 **N** Bus: 10

Lumière £££ This haute cuisine temple is a tiny (seats about 40) room with exquisite formal service, divine West Coast-inflected French cuisine and a renowned wine list. ⓐ 2551 W Broadway ⓣ 604-739-8185 ⓦ www.lumiere.ca ⓛ 17.30–23.00 Wed–Sun ⓝ Bus: 9

Tojo's £££ Indisputably the best sushi in Vancouver is served at the namesake restaurant of chef Hidekazu Tojo, a city institution for 35 years. Sit at the sushi bar for an *omakase* dining experience you will never forget, or book a private *tatami* room for your group. ⓐ 1133 W Broadway ⓣ 604-872-8050 ⓛ 17.30–00.00 Mon–Sat ⓝ Bus: 9

West £££ Pacific Northwest cuisine at its best is the hallmark of this sophisticated South Granville restaurant, which has one of the best mixologists in the city behind the bar. ⓐ 2881 Granville St ⓣ 604-738-8938 ⓦ www.westrestaurant.com ⓛ 11.30–14.00, 17.30–23.00 Mon–Fri, 17.30–23.00 Sat & Sun ⓝ Bus: 10

BARS & PUBS

Sandbar The semi-covered deck, complete with cosy firepit, at this Granville Island seafood restaurant is a wonderful spot for a drink overlooking False Creek. ⓐ 1535 Johnston St ⓣ 604-669-9030 ⓛ 11.30–15.00, 17.00–22.00 Sun–Thur, 17.00–23.00 Fri & Sat ⓝ Bus: 50

Watermark Watching the sunset from the covered patio overlooking Kitsilano Beach is the perfect end to a summer night in Vancouver. ⓐ 1305 Arbutus St ⓣ 604-738-5487 ⓦ www.watermarkrestaurant.ca ⓛ 11.30–00.00 Mon–Fri, 11.00–00.00 Sat & Sun ⓝ Bus: 2, 22

CINEMAS

Vancouver's vintage movie theatres, while somewhat lacking in lustre, have character to spare. The vintage **Ridge** (⊜ 3131 Arbutus St ❶ 604-732-3352 ⊗ Bus: 16) and **Park** (⊜ 3440 Cambie St ❶ 604-709-3456 ⊗ Bus: 15, 33) theatres, along with the modern **Fifth Avenue Cinemas** (⊜ 2110 Burrard St ❶ 604-734-7469 ⊗ Bus: 4, 44) play first-run alternative, foreign and Hollywood movies. For film times, see ⓦ www.festivalcinemas.ca.

⬤ Check out the fabulous Watermark bar and restaurant

East Side

Don't limit your explorations of Vancouver to its shiny glass-towered Downtown or gentrified West Side sectors – the East Side of the city is where in-the-know locals live, work and play these days. The emerging areas, including the Main Street and Commercial Drive corridors, are increasingly seeing new restaurants and shops rub elbows with old neighbourhood joints like coffee shops and pool halls. The pace is relaxed, the fashions are streetwise and the locals are friendly. The lack of built attractions means you won't see many other tourists, but you'll get a glimpse of the real everyday life of Vancouver's young, hip creative set by hanging out here. A bonus: the prices, for everything from food to entertainment, are small-town instead of big-city.

SIGHTS & ATTRACTIONS

Trout Lake

One of Vancouver's first sawmills was located on this charming lake, now a city park with a community centre offering ice skating in winter and a fitness centre throughout the year. From May to October, attend the **Saturday Farmers' Market** (ⓦ www.eatlocal.org) and walk off the calories from your purchases with a stroll around the lake. ⓐ Victoria Drive & 15th Ave ⓦ www.vancouver.ca

Vancouver Specials tour

The Vancouver Special is the defining housing style of the formerly working class East Side neighbourhoods. Displaying an oddball amalgamation of architectural styles seen nowhere else in the

⬥ *Autumn colour in Trout Lake park*

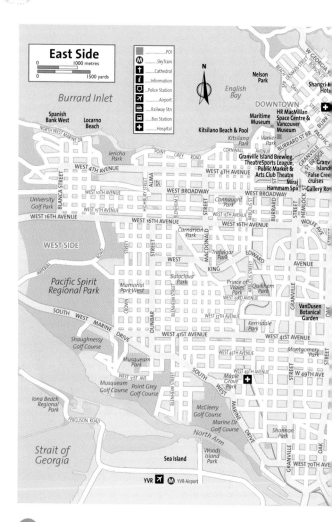

East Side

0 _____ 1000 metres
0 _____ 1500 yards

M	POI
T	SkyTrain
i	Cathedral
	Information
	Police Station
	Airport
	Railway Stn
	Bus Station
+	Hospital

N

Burrard Inlet

English Bay

Nelson Park

Shangri-L Hote

DOWNTOWN

Spanish Bank West

Locarno Beach

Maritime Museum

HR MacMillan Space Centre & Vancouver Museum

NORTH WEST MARINE DR

Kitsilano Beach & Pool

Jericho Park

POINT GREY ROAD

CORNWALL

Kitsilano Park

Vanier Park

BURRARD ST BR

PACIFIC

WEST 4TH AVENUE

WEST 4TH AVENUE

Granville Island Brewing, TheatreSports League, Public Market & Arts Club Theatre

Granville Island

GRANVILLE

ST BRIDGE

BURR

WEST BROADWAY

WEST BROADWAY

Miraj Hammam Spa

False Creek cruises

Gallery Ro

University Golf Park

BLANCA STREET

ALMA ST

HIGHBURY STREET

BLENHEIM STREET

WEST 10TH AVENUE

Connaught Park

WEST BROADWAY

BURRARD STREET

HEMLOCK

WOLFE AVE

WEST 15TH AVENUE

WEST 15TH AVENUE

WEST 16TH AVENUE

WEST 16TH AVENUE

WEST 16TH AVENUE

Carnarvon Park

MACDONALD

WEST SIDE

IMPERIAL ROAD

STREET

STREET

Trafalgar Park

EDWARD

WEST

KING

AVENUE

Pacific Spirit Regional Park

Balaclava Park

Prince of Wales Park

Quilchem Park

GRANVILLE

Mamorial Park West

WEST 33RD AVENUE

VanDusen Botanical Garden

OAK

CROWN

DUNBAR

BLENHEIM STREET

WEST 37TH AVENUE

SOUTH WEST MARINE DRIVE

Kerrisdale Park

Shaughnessy Golf Course

WEST 41ST AVENUE

WEST 41ST AVENUE

Montgomery Park

STREET

Musqueam Park

WEST 45TH AVENUE

WEST 49TH AVENUE

W 49TH AVE

Musqueam Golf Course

Point Grey Golf Course

WEST 51ST AVE

BLENHEIM STREET

SOUTH

Maple Grove Park

+

Iona Beach Regional Park

McCleery Golf Course

WEST MARINE DRIVE

GRANVILLE

FERGUSON ROAD

Marine Dr Golf Course

Shannon Park

North Arm

Strait of Georgia

Woods Island Park

WEST 70TH AVE

Sea Island

YVR ✈ M YVR-Airport

world, these so-called 'Specials' are now being reclaimed and renovated by hip young families, who are gentrifying the surrounding neighbourhoods with great shopping and eating possibilities. Tours and showcases of Vancouver Specials have become a popular attraction of the design-conscious. For more information and tour times, call ☏ 604-264-9642 or check ⓦ www.vancouverheritagefoundation.org.

CULTURE

Catriona Jeffries Gallery

A neighbouring gallery to Elliot Lewis, the intriguing space specialises in daring post-conceptual contemporary art.
ⓐ 274 E 1st Ave ☏ 604-736-1554 ⓦ www.catrionajeffries.com
🕐 11.00–17.00 Tues–Sat Ⓝ Bus: 84

Eastside Cultural Centre

Affectionately known as 'The Cultch,' this artistic community hub, located in a former church, is one of the city's most beloved live music venues. Dance performances, family entertainment, plays and musical theatre are among the offerings in a typical season.
ⓐ 1895 Venables St ☏ 604-251-1363 ⓦ www.thecultch.com Ⓝ Bus: 3

Elliot Louis Gallery

A fine art gallery specialising in Canadian art which made the brave move from West Side to East Side, where many of its cutting-edge artists and their clients no doubt live. ⓐ 258 E 1st Ave
☏ 604-736-3282 ⓦ www.elliotlouis.com 🕐 10.00–18.00 Tues–Sat
Ⓝ Bus: 84

▲ The classic art deco-style Heritage Hall is host to many public events

PORTOBELLO WEST MARKET

On the last Sunday of every month, an eclectic group of artisans, craftspeople and local fashionistas gather in the Rocky Mountaineer train station to hawk their one-of-a-kind wares, many of them with an organic, sustainable or recycled bent. It's best to go for the experience, rather than for any serious shopping. 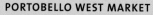 1775 Cottrell St, off Terminal Ave 🕸 www.vancouver.portobellowest.com 🕒 12.00–18.00 last Sun of month, Mar–Dec 🄽 SkyTrain: Science World-Main Street

Heritage Hall

The beautiful c. 1915 former post office building at the corner of Main and 15th Avenue is lovingly restored and maintained by its own Preservation Society, which rents it out for special events and functions. From the sidewalk, admire the exterior sandstone carvings and vintage mechanical clock and bell. Weekend craft fairs or other public events offer a chance to peek inside – check events listings for what's on. 🄰 3102 Main St 🄣 604-879-4816 🕸 www.heritagehall.bc.ca 🄽 Bus: 3

RETAIL THERAPY

Attic Treasures Western Canada is a treasure trove of mid-century modern furnishings, and this store has a good selection, including colourful tableware, lamps and kitschy pop-culture accessories. 🄰 944 Commercial Drive 🄣 604-254-0220 🕒 11.00–18.00 🄽 Bus: 20

Eugene Choo Men's and women's clothing and accessories are showcased in this store, with everything from hoodies and cool t-shirts to suits and handmade shoes. ⓐ 3683 Main St ① 604-873-8874 ⓦ www.eugenechoo.com ⓛ 11.00–19.00 Mon–Fri, 11.00–18.00 Sat, 12.00–17.00 Sun Ⓝ Bus: 3

Gourmet Warehouse Amateur cooks and serious foodies will want to spend time browsing this big, warehouse-style store for quality gadgets and foodstuffs, which has just about everything from locally made kitchen cleaning products to probably the city's best selection of cake and baking supplies. ⓐ 1340 E Hastings St ① 604-253-3022 ⓦ www.gourmetwarehouse.ca ⓛ 10.00–18.00 Mon–Sat, 10.00–17.00 Sun Ⓝ Bus: 10, 16

Jonathan and Olivia This boutique has the latest lines for women and men who like a polished, urban look, including coveted lines like Malin & Goetz and Opening Ceremony. Long-time fashion insider Jackie O'Brien hand-picks all the stock and the store offers service perks like free hemming, private shopping, worldwide mail order and layaway service. ⓐ 2570 Main St ① 604-637-6224 ⓦ www.jonathanandolivia.com ⓛ 11.00–19.00 Mon–Fri, 11.00–18.00 Sat, 12.00–17.00 Sun Ⓝ Bus: 3

Lark A white, minimalist store selling cutting-edge international fashion for men and women as well as jewellery from local darlings Pyrrha, a company that makes delicate pendants imprinted with designs from vintage wax seals. ⓐ 2315 Main St ① 604-879-5275 ⓦ www.lark.me ⓛ 11.00–18.00 Mon–Thur, 11.00–19.00 Fri & Sat, 12.00–17.00 Sun Ⓝ Bus: 3

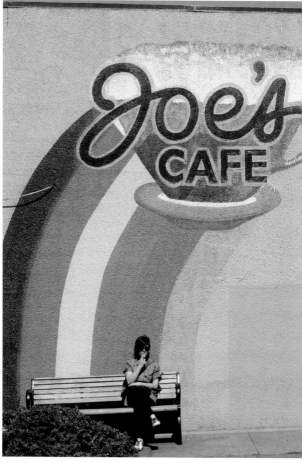

○ Take a break at the eclectic Joe's Café

Mountain Equipment Co-op If a camping or hiking trip is coming up, stop at this top Canadian emporium for all things outdoorsy. Its house brand is surprisingly well priced, staff are extremely knowledgeable and the company prides itself on ethical sourcing and business practices. Since it's a co-operative, you'll need to sign up for a $5 membership to make purchases. ⓐ 130 W Broadway ⓣ 604-872-7858 ⓦ www.mec.ca ⓛ 10.00–19.00 Mon–Wed, 10.00–21.00 Thur & Fri, 09.00–18.00 Sat, 11.00–17.00 Sun ⓝ Bus: 8, 9

Retro Rock Vintage Clothing This treasure trove of styles from days gone by – that are always coming back – yields plenty of fashion scores. ⓐ 2240 Commercial Drive ⓣ 604-872-7670 ⓛ 11.00–18.00 ⓝ Bus: 20

Twigg&hottie A focus on sustainable fashion makes this quirky store one-stop shopping for organic cotton, silk clothing and unique jewellery. ⓐ 3671 Main St ⓣ 604-879-8595 ⓦ www.twiggandhottie.com ⓛ 11.00–18.00 Mon–Thur, 11.00–19.00 Fri & Sat, 12.00–17.00 Sun ⓝ Bus: 3

TAKING A BREAK

Joe's Café £ ❶ At this vintage café and pool hall, the espresso drinks are terrific and the sandwiches, made with crusty Portuguese buns, are simple but delicious. ⓐ 1150 Commercial Drive ⓣ 604-255-1046 ⓦ www.joescafebar.com ⓛ 08.00–00.00 ⓝ Bus: 20

Liberty Bakery £ ❷ With the look of an old corner store, this warm neighbourhood bakery has a few tables for enjoying its

pastries, light (soup and sandwich) lunches and sugary treats.
ⓐ 3699 Main St ⓣ 604-709-9999 ⓛ 08.00–18.00 Wed–Mon,
08.00–16.00 Tues ⓝ Bus: 3

SoMa £ ❸ Named for the 'hood it helped popularise (SoMa
stands for South Main), the original neighbourhood café
has since moved to a new location just off the Main Street
strip, and is now an all-day restaurant and bar that's still a
crowd-pleasing favourite. ⓐ 151 E 8th Ave ⓣ 604-630-7502
ⓛ 09.00–01.00 Mon–Sat, 09.00–00.00 Sun ⓝ Bus: 3

Crave on Main ££ ❹ Scrambled eggs with savoury short rib for
breakfast, an organic beef burger for lunch or hearty braised lamb
shank for dinner are among the options at this all-day restaurant.
ⓐ 3941 Main St ⓣ 604-872-3663 ⓦ www.craverestaurants.com
ⓛ 11.00–22.00 Mon–Fri, 09.00–22.00 Sat, 09.00–21.00 Sun ⓝ Bus: 3

Au Petit Chavignol ££ ❺ A wine, cheese and charcuterie
restaurant and bar run by the proprietors of the city's best cheese
shops, offering fondue and raclette as well as platters of artisan
meat, cheese and pâté. ⓐ 843 E Hastings St ⓣ 604-255-4218
ⓦ www.aupetitchavignol.com ⓛ 17.00–23.00 ⓝ Bus: 10, 16

AFTER DARK

RESTAURANTS
Campagnolo ££ ❻ The restaurateurs behind Fuel (see page 86)
created this cheap, chic Italian joint in an underserviced
neighbourhood and the place has been packing in the

crowds ever since. Crispy pizzas, rustic pastas and homemade charcuterie are highlights. **a** 1020 Main St **t** 604-484-6018 **w** www.campagnolorestaurant.ca **c** 11.00–22.00 Sun–Thur, 11.00–23.00 Fri & Sat **n** SkyTrain: Science World-Main Street

Les Faux Bourgeois ££ ❼ In an unlikely location – a dowdy strip mall off the Kingsway thoroughfare – this stylish little restaurant looks like a vintage recreation room but serves food which tastes like it comes from a classic Parisian bistro. **a** 663 E 15th Ave **t** 604-873-9733 **w** www.lesfauxbourgeois.com **c** 17.30–00.00 Tues–Sun **n** Bus: 19

Me and Julio ££ ❽ Mexican food abounds on Commercial Drive, and this place is the most popular, especially for its ceviches of local seafood and big pitchers of sangria. **a** 2095 Commercial Drive **t** 604-696-9997 **w** www.meandjulio.ca **c** 16.00–00.00 **n** Bus: 20

Ping's Café ££ ❾ The décor has as much cachet as the food here, with design elements by local star Omer Arbel and a big Rodney Graham painting on a back wall. The culinary style is *yoshuku*, American diner food as interpreted by Japanese cafés. **a** 2702 Main St **t** 604-873-2702 **w** www.pingscafe.ca **c** 17.00–22.30 Tues–Thur, 17.00–00.00 Fri & Sat **n** Bus: 3

Reef ££ ❿ The city's standout Caribbean food purveyor is famous for jerk chicken and Jamaica's benchmark meal of ackee fruit, salt cod, rice and peas. **a** 4172 Main St **t** 604-874-5375 **w** www.thereefrestaurant.com **c** 11.00–23.00 Mon–Wed, 11.00–00.00 Thur & Fri, 10.00–00.00 Sat, 10.00–23.00 Sun **n** Bus: 20

BARS

Cascade Reinventing the traditional English pub, this bar created by award-winning interior design firm Evoke has a great, cheap wine list, good cocktails and hearty pub food like burgers and chips. ⓐ 2616 Main St ⓣ 604-709-8650 ⓦ www.thecascade.ca ⓛ 16.00–00.00 Mon–Fri, 12.00–00.00 Sat & Sun ⓝ Bus: 3

Five Point Live music on stage, hockey games on the TV, cheap beer prices: everything a good pub needs. There's a nice outdoor patio in summer. ⓐ 3124 Main St ⓣ 604-876-5810 ⓛ 16.00–00.00 Mon–Fri, 12.00–00.00 Sat & Sun ⓝ Bus: 3

Havana A bohemian enclave (there's a gallery in the back, and frequent readings, live music and other events) with great Latin-style food. ⓐ 1212 Commercial Drive ⓣ 604-253-9119 ⓦ www.havanarestaurant.ca ⓛ 11.00–00.00 Mon–Thur, 11.00–01.00 Fri & Sat ⓝ Bus: 20

Narrow Lounge You'll feel like you've discovered a secret speakeasy when you enter the unmarked door under the red light and descend a dark stairway to this closet-size bar. Classic cocktails and a small menu of tasty snacks mean that those lucky enough to grab a barstool stay a while. ⓐ 1898 Main St ⓣ No phone ⓦ www.narrowlounge.com ⓛ 17.00–01.00 ⓝ Bus: 3

ⓓ *The beautiful Butchart Gardens just out of Victoria are worth a visit*

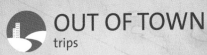

OUT OF TOWN
trips

Whistler

A weekend playground for Vancouverites and American visitors, Whistler finally got the international recognition it deserved as host location of the alpine events for the 2010 Winter Olympics. World-class skiing and snowboarding – you can traverse more than 200 runs, 13 bowls and eight glaciers from November to June – as well as ice climbing, cross-country skiing, snowmobiling, snowshoeing and snow tubing are among the ways to enjoy the snowy months. In summer, the ski trails make for challenging mountain biking. Other warm-weather outdoor activities include rock climbing, zip-lining and paddling sports. Every November, the **Cornucopia** (ⓦ www.whistlercornucopia.com) food and wine festival sees the best of the world's wines paired with the local culinary scene – just one indication of how sophisticated Whistler's après-ski scene has become.

Whistler Activities & Information Centre ⓐ 4010 Whistler Way
ⓣ 604-938-2769 ⓦ www.whistler.com

GETTING THERE

Hunker down for a luxe three-hour train trip between Vancouver and Whistler on the **Whistler Mountaineer** (ⓣ 604-606-8460 ⓦ www.whistlermountaineer.com), through stunning mountain vistas and old-growth forest best viewed from the clear-roofed Glacier Dome car. The Whistler station is in Creekside, and a shuttle will take you right into Whistler Village. Driving will take at least two and a half hours, sometimes longer depending on traffic and weather conditions. **SkyLynx** (ⓣ 604-662-7575

 Looking down the ski slopes of Whistler

Around Vancouver

0 — 25 miles
0 — 35 kilometres

Lilooet Lake

Lillooet Range

CANADA

Mount Zakwaski
▲ 2058

Aspen Grove

Boston Bar

BRITISH COLUMBIA

Spuzzum

Yale

Dogwood Valley

Harrison Lake

Princeton

Stave Lake

Harrison Hot Springs

Harrison Mill

Kent

Hope

Maple Ridge

Mission

Chilliwack

Bridal Falls

Skagit Mountain
2356
Silvertip Mountain
▲ 2606

Abbotsford
Huntingdon

Sumas

nden

Everson

Manning Park

Deming

Mount Baker
▲ 3285

llingham

Baker Lake

U.S.A.
North Cascades National Park

Ross Lake

Vancouver

Diablo

lanchard

WASHINGTON

Lyman

Concrete

North Cascades National Park

Mount Logan
▲ 2733

Goode Mountain
▲ 2784

Sedro-Woolley

Skagit

Mount Vernon

Rockport

○	City
○	Large Town
○	Small Town
■	POI
	Motorway
	Main Road
	Minor Road
✈	Airport
	Railway

www.pacificcoach.com) runs shuttle buses to Whistler from the airport and Downtown, with the three-hour trip costing approximately $50 each way.

SIGHTS & ATTRACTIONS

Peak 2 Peak Gondola

Spanning a world record-breaking 4.4 km (2¾ miles) between Whistler and Blackcomb peaks, and reaching a height of 435 m (1427 ft) above the ground, this modern tram unites two superb ski areas in winter. In summer, it takes you to more than 50 km (31 miles) of idyllic hiking trails. The view from the tramcar makes for outstanding 360-degree sightseeing all year round. ⓐ 4545 Blackcomb Way ❶ 888-218-9684 ⓦ www.whistlerblackcomb.com ◷ Hours vary by season. Admission charge

Solarice Spa

Though there are any number of places to get a post-activity rubdown in Whistler, Solarice stands out from the rest for its focus on natural and organic product lines (like Eminence from Hungary) and naturopathic treatments incorporating Chinese traditional medicine and more. Yoga and pilates classes are also offered. ⓐ 4230 Gateway Drive Suite 202 ❶ 604-935-1222 ⓦ www.solarice.com ◷ 09.00–19.00 Sun–Wed, 09.00–20.00 Fri & Sat

Whistler Bike Park

Riders rave about the latest addition to the Garbanzo zone, 2,200 vertical feet of single-track trails (on top of an existing 1,200 vertical feet). Riders take the gondola up and can spend

FIRST NATIONS

Whether it's soapstone carvings, Cowichan sweaters, Haida Gwai jewellery or smoked salmon, Whistler's galleries and shops are filled with products inspired and created by West Coast indigenous culture. (Note that the 'First Nations' is the politically correct term – never, ever use 'Indian'.) A few recommended Whistler stops include **West Coast Gallery** (ⓐ 4320 Sundial Cres. ① 604-935-0087), which specialises in art, jewellery, silver and soapstone; **Black Tusk Gallery** (ⓐ 4293 Mountain Square Suite 108 ① 877-905-5540), which features masks, carvings, totem poles, jewellery, prints); and **Path Gallery** (ⓐ 4388 Main St Suite 122 ① 604-932-7570), which has masks, paddles, drums, carved boxes and sculptures.

anything from 15 minutes to an hour negotiating their way down rugged mountain terrain on two wheels. Rentals (🕔 09.30–20.00) are available in the Village Gondola Building at the foot of the mountain. ⓐ 4545 Blackcomb Way ① 888-218-9684 ⓦ www.whistlerblackcomb.com 🕔 10.00–17.00; hours vary by season. Admission charge

Whistler Farmers' Market

The nearby agricultural area of Pemberton is the larder for this fresh produce market, which takes place every Sunday from late June through early October. Music, entertainment and snacks are part of the tasty package. ⓐ Chateau Blvd, b/n Fairmont Chateau

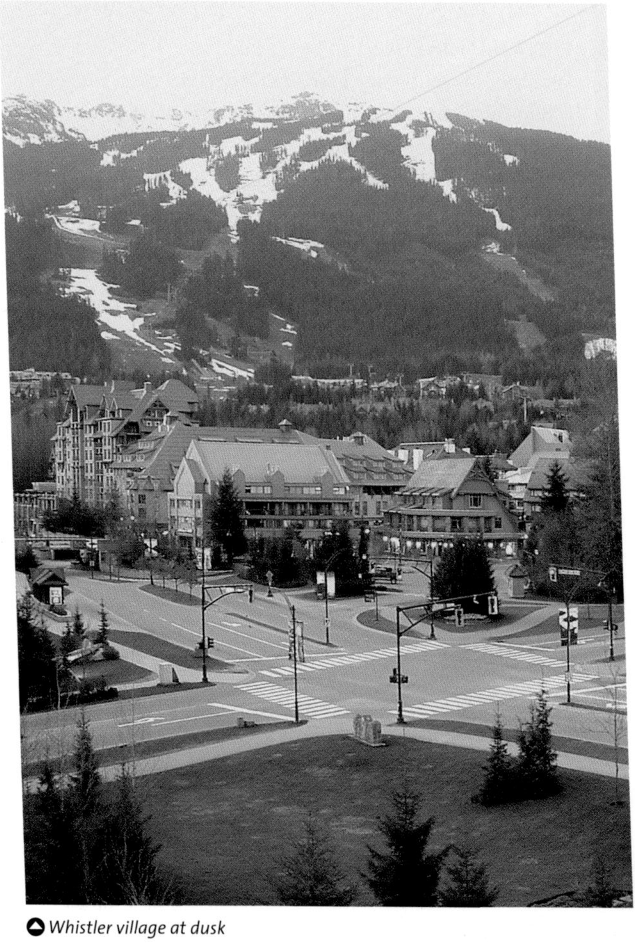

Whistler village at dusk

Whistler & Glacier Lodge ⓦ www.whistlerfarmersmarket.org
🕐 11.00–16.00 Sun, late June–early Oct

Ziptrek Ecotours

If flying down a cable hanging from a harness is your idea of fun, these tours through stretches of old-growth rainforest between the Whistler and Blackcomb peaks will be right up your alley. Certain tours focus on bear or eagle watching, while others are purely about adrenaline-pumping fun. ⓐ Office: Carleton Lodge, opposite Whistler Gondola building ⓣ 604-935-0001 ⓦ www.ziptrek.com.

CULTURE

Squamish Lil'Wat Cultural Centre

The two native cultures of this region (the Squamish and Lil'Wat people) united to create this showcase of traditions ranging from song and dance to storytelling and craft to food. The architecture of the contemporary building innovatively combines the hallmarks of a native longhouse and traditional pit dwelling. ⓐ 4584 Blackcomb Way ⓣ 604-964-0990 ⓦ www.slcc.ca 🕐 09.30–17.00. Admission charge

Whistler Museum & Archives

The history of Whistler's once-humble mountain community, now turned jet-set ski retreat, is chronicled here, in striking images and exhibits relating to the natural and built history of the area. ⓐ 4333 Main St ⓣ 604-932-2019 🕐 11.00–16.00 Wed–Sat. Admission charge

RETAIL THERAPY

Armchair Books Whether it's a stunning photo essay on the region or a dishy novel you want to escape into, the village bookshop has the full range of options, including sporting and travel guides. ⓐ 4201 Village Square ⓣ 604-932-5557 ⓦ www.whistlerbooks.com ⓛ 09.00–21.00

Burton Women's Store The only female-specific Burton outlet in the world, this boutique (within the Sundial Whistler Hotel) features the size ranges, designs and accessories suited to stylish board bunnies. ⓐ 4340 Sundial Crescent ⓛ 09.00–21.00

Rocky Mountain Chocolate Factory Fudge, candy apples, filled chocolates, flavoured popcorn and ice cream are a few of the tempting delights you'll see prepared through the glass storefront of this staple of Canadian mountain resorts. A selection of sugar-free treats are perfect for diabetics and dieters. ⓐ 4293 Mountain Square ⓣ 604-932-4100 ⓦ www.rockychoc.com ⓛ 09.00–21.00

Whistler Blackcomb Outlet Store Located just down the slope in Squamish, this clearance outlet for ski, snowboard and outdoor sport equipment features up to 70 per cent off regular prices. ⓐ Garibaldi Village, Garibaldi Way at Hwy 99 ⓣ 604-898-3115 ⓛ 09.00–21.00

TAKING A BREAK

Avalanche Pizza £ The smells coming from this pizzeria are enough to draw you in – and given that the pizza dough is made with organic ingredients, it's practically good for you. Salads, garlic bread and beverages round out the menu. ⓐ 4295 Blackcomb Way Suite 109 ⓣ 604-932-3131 ⓦ www.avalanchepizza.com ⓛ 11.00–23.00

BBQ Bob's £ Located within Roland's pub, just steps from the Rocky Mountaineer train station in Creekside, the home of one of the area's top barbecue competition champions smokes great ribs, pulled pork, chicken and beef. Meals are extremely hearty, so prepare to have leftovers. ⓐ 2129 Lake Placid Rd ⓣ 604-932-4424 ⓦ www.rolandswhistler.com ⓛ 11.00–22.00

Beat Root Café £ For homemade sandwiches, soups and stews, fresh-baked treats and hearty breakfasts (including vegetarian options), this cosy café is a favourite with locals. ⓐ 4340 Lorimer Rd ⓣ 604-932-1163 ⓛ 07.30–18.00 Mon–Wed & Sun, 07.30–21.00 Fri & Sat

AFTER DARK

RESTAURANTS
Araxi £££+ The prize for the winning contestant in a recent series of *Hell's Kitchen* was a job here, at the most acclaimed restaurant in Whistler. ⓐ 4222 Village Square ⓣ 604-932-4540 ⓦ www.araxi.com ⓛ 11.30–15.00, 17.00–00.00

Bearfoot Bistro £££+ Canada's chef of the year in 2008 was the young female toque, Melissa Craig, who runs this restaurant

where your champagne can be flamboyantly opened with a sabre.
ⓐ 4121 Village Green ⓣ 604-932-3433 ⓦ www.bearfootbistro.com
ⓛ 17.30–00.00

BARS & CLUBS

Whistler Village bars compete for the biggest patio, coldest
beer and rowdiest crowds. Among the favourite watering
holes are **Garfinkel's** (ⓐ 4308 Main St ⓣ 604-932-2323
ⓦ www.garfswhistler.com ⓛ 21.00–02.00), **Dusty's Bar &
BBQ** (ⓐ 2040 London Lane ⓣ 604-905-2146 ⓛ 11.00–01.00),
Garibaldi Lift Company (ⓐ 4165 Springs Lane ⓣ 604-905-2220
ⓛ 11.00–01.00) and the **Longhorn Saloon** (ⓐ 4284 Mountain Square
ⓣ 604-932-5999 ⓦ www.longhornsaloon.ca ⓛ 09.00–01.00).
There are also a few clubs to get your groove on, mostly drawing
a younger crowd. **Maxx Fish** (ⓐ 4232 Village Stroll ⓣ 604-932-1904
ⓦ www.maxxfish.moonfruit.com ⓛ 09.00–02.00 Tues–Sat),
Tommy Africa's (ⓐ 4216 Gateway Drive ⓣ 604-932-6090
ⓦ www.tommyafricas.com ⓛ 21.00–02.00 Tues–Sat 21.00–00.00
Sun) and the **Savage Beagle** (ⓐ 4222 Village Square ⓣ 604-938-3337
ⓦ www.savagebeagle.com ⓛ 09.30–02.00) are the most
popular DJ-driven dance scenes.

Fifty Two 80 The elegant bar at the Four Seasons Whistler Resort
makes a killer Bloody Caesar and has a tasty snack menu – it's
not cheap, but you can linger in front of the cosy fireplace in a
comfortable armchair. ⓐ 4591 Blackcomb Way ⓣ 604-935-3400
ⓛ 12.00–00.00

CINEMA

Village 8 Cinemas Current releases are shown on eight big screens at this movie theatre right in the village, a good option for a rainy day or quiet night. ⓐ 4295 Blackcomb Way ⓣ 604-932-5833 ⓦ www.village8.ca

ACCOMMODATION

Adara Hotel ££ A sister property to the stylish Opus Hotel in Vancouver's Yaletown, this chic boutique hotel has great loft-style suites and cosy rooms. The location is great, just far enough (but not too far) away from the village bustle, and there's a great outdoor pool in summer. ⓐ 4122 Village Green ⓣ 866-502-3272 ⓦ www.adarahotel.com

Four Seasons Whistler £££ Luxury has a price, but the outdoor hot tubs, deluxe gym and spa, well-appointed marble bathrooms and tiptop concierge service (they'll even outfit you in Prada ski gear in winter) makes this the best hotel in Whistler, hands down. Close to the famed Nicklaus North Golf Course. ⓐ 4591 Blackcomb Way ⓣ 604-935-3400 ⓦ www.fourseasons.com

Victoria

Victoria, the capital of British Columbia and the largest city on Vancouver Island, is a genteel and British-inflected city with an easy walkable and navigable Downtown core around the Inner Harbour. Though it's not a party town for late nights or clubbing, in recent years Victoria has developed a dynamite food scene and a thriving clutch of interesting boutiques selling locally made goods. **Victoria Visitor Centre** ⓐ 812 Wharf St ⓣ 250-953-2033 ⓦ www.tourismvictoria.com ⓛ 09.00–17.00

GETTING THERE

Located about 80 kilometres from Vancouver across the Strait of Georgia, Vancouver Island is an easy day trip by ferry with **BC Ferries** (ⓦ www.bcferries.com). A one-way adult ticket costs around $13.50 for the one and a half hour journey and a vehicle adds another $45 to the total fare. **Pacific Coach** (ⓦ www.pacificcoach.com) offers bus trips by ferry between Vancouver and Victoria, taking just under four hours and costing around $43 per adult one-way. Float plane is the quickest (35 minutes) and most convenient option, especially if it takes you from one Downtown harbour to another rather than to and from the airports: try **West Coast Air** (ⓦ www.westcoastair.com), **Harbour Air** (ⓦ www.harbour-air.com) or **Seair Seaplanes** (ⓦ www.seairseaplanes.com). The cost is upwards of $134 each way, not including tax. The **Helijet** (ⓦ www.helijet.com) terminal in Victoria is a slightly less convenient location but a fun and zippy option.

⬥ Promenade along Victoria's harbourside

SIGHTS & ATTRACTIONS

Whale-watching tours

From Victoria's Inner Harbour, about a dozen companies offer whale-watching tours by Zodiac (can be choppy) or ocean cruiser (more smooth and sedate), complete with all the gear you'll need to stay dry and safe. The season is March to October, with peak orca viewing in June and July and plenty of grey whales, seals, sea lions and sea birds during the other months. The visitor centre (see page 116) can advise on tour companies and has a good directory on its website.

Wine & culinary tours

The fertile Saanich Peninsula and Cowichan Valley are within striking distance of Victoria, so consider a day trip to some **wineries** (Ⓦ www.verjuswinetours.com) or **foodie hotspots** (Ⓦ www.travelwithtaste.com) while on Vancouver Island. There are also a number of local breweries that offers tours and tastings, including **Phillips Brewing Company** (ⓐ 2010 Government St ① 250-380-1912 Ⓦ www.phillipsbeer.com), makers of great IPAs and porters, and **Vancouver Island Brewery** (ⓐ 2330 Government St ① 250-361-0005 Ⓦ www.vanislandbrewery.com).

CULTURE

Antique Row

Along Fort Street, at least a dozen shops specialise in china and silver, military memorabilia, art and antique furniture. You can get a good walking tour map and directory from the tourist

BUTCHART GARDENS

Victoria's world-renowned botanical garden has been recognised as a National Historic Site of Canada and is still owned by descendants of the family that created it more than a century ago. The 55 acre (22 hectare) parcel just outside Victoria is worth the trip, as it's a lovely picnic and strolling destination all year round. Spring brings a riot of tulips and daffodils, summer sees fireworks displays every Saturday and in winter there's an outdoor skating rink. Two restaurants and a coffee shop within the gardens feature homemade specialities like Italian sausage and chocolate truffles, while afternoon tea includes lemon poppyseed loaf made to a family recipe. ⓐ 800 Benvenuto Ave ⓣ 250-652-4422 ⓦ www.butchartgardens.com ⓛ 09.00–21.00 (hours vary). Admission charge

office, and it makes a great theme for a stroll even if you're not intending to buy.

Art Gallery of Greater Victoria

Particularly known for its collections of Asian art (notably its Japanese collection, including an authentic Shinto shrine), the gallery is located in a heritage building in Rockland, a stately neighbourhood a short distance from the Inner Harbour. ⓐ 1040 Moss St ⓣ 250-384-4101 ⓦ www.aggv.bc.ca ⓛ 10.00–17.00 Mon–Wed, Fri & Sat, 10.00–21.00 Thur, 12.00–17.00 Sun. Admission charge

⬥ *Victoria's Parliament building sparkles at night*

Maritime Museum of British Columbia

From early explorers to pirates and fabled shipwrecks, the exhibits and artefacts on display here – including vintage ships – tell the whole coastal history of the area. ⓐ 28 Bastion Square ⓣ 250-385-4222 ⓦ www.mmbc.bc.ca ⓛ 09.30–18.00 (hours vary). Admission charge

Royal BC Museum

An interactive gallery containing a rainforest simulation, displays on natural history and an overview of First Nations culture on the coast of British Columbia. ⓐ 675 Belleville St ⓣ 250-356-7226 ⓦ www.royalbcmuseum.bc.ca ⓛ 09.00–22.00 summer; 09.00–17.00 winter. Admission charge

RETAIL THERAPY

Rogers' Chocolate Founded in Victoria in 1885, this old-timey chocolate store is generous with sample tastings and offers gorgeously boxed souvenir treats. Just down the block at 801 Government Street is the old-fashioned Rogers' Chocolate Soda Shoppe, with its signature Capital City Banana Split, made using Rogers ice cream. ⓐ 913 Government St ⓣ 250-881-8771 ⓦ www.rogerschocolates.com ⓛ 09.30–20.00 Mon–Thur, 09.30–21.00 Fri & Sat, 10.00–20.00 Sun

Silk Road Tea Run by experts trained by Chinese herbalists and tea specialists, this Chinatown shop sells not only exquisite tea blends but also unique serving accessories and tea-infused body products. There is a spa (with tea-based treatments) located on site. Daily tastings take place at 14.00 during the summer months; workshops range from making tea-based perfumes to blending tea-flavoured cocktails. ⓐ 1624 Government St ⓣ 250-704-2688 ⓦ www.silkroadtea.com ⓛ 10.00–18.00 Mon–Sat, 11.00–17.00 Sun

Smoking Lily This local company has made a big name for itself with original designs of silkscreened scarves, bags, men's and women's t-shirts and household goods like pillows and tea towels. ⓐ 569A Johnson St ⓣ 250-382-5459 ⓦ www.smokinglily.com ⓛ 11.00–17.30 Tues–Sat, 12.00–17.00 Sun & Mon

TAKING A BREAK

Choux Choux Charcuterie £ A deli featuring homemade cured meats, top European cheeses, artisan bread from local baker House Breads, savoury pies, and all the fixing you'll need – from crackers to olives – to put together a great picnic. Alternatively, if you can find a space, eat at one of the tables in the shop or on the sidewalk. ⓐ 830 Fort St ⓣ 250-382-7572 ⓦ www.chouxchoux.ca ⓛ 10.00–17.30 Tues–Fri, 10.00–17.00 Sat

Daidoco £ This Japanese lunch spot makes yummy rice bowls, salads and baked goods that are a favourite of the weekday office crowd. ⓐ Nootka Court, 633 Courtney St ⓣ 250-388-7383 ⓛ 10.00–18.00 Mon–Fri

Dutch Bakery & Coffee Shop £ Still trapped in an authentic bubble of mid-1950s nostalgia, this charming family bakery and café has cheap prices on breakfast and lunch meals and a tempting bakery and chocolate selection, including apple pie, strudel and intricate little cookies. ⓐ 718 Fort St ⓣ 250-385-1012 ⓒ 07.30–17.30 Tues–Sat

Pig BBQ Joint £ They do one thing, and do it extremely well: sandwiches made of meat (beef, chicken, or pork) that has been smoked into submission. Excellent cornbread, beans, coleslaw and dill pickles are among the optional accompaniments. ⓐ 749 View St ⓣ 250-381-4677 ⓦ www.pigbbqjoint.com ⓒ 11.00–17.00 Mon, 11.00–18.30 Tues–Sat

Mo:Le ££ Chef Cosmo Meens cooks for the Canadian Olympic triathlon team, which tells you he knows how to make filling, delicious and above all healthy food. Hearty breakfasts are sided with pesto-flavoured hash brown potatoes and the sausages from local purveyor Galloping Goose are fantastic. ⓐ 554 Pandora Ave ⓣ 250-385-6653 ⓦ www.molerestaurant.ca ⓒ 08.00–15.00 Mon–Fri, 08.00–16.00 Sat & Sun

Re-bar ££ A healthy food joint and juice bar which has become so popular during its 20-year life that it has now published its own cookbook. Famous for stir-fries, salads and pastas cooked with local produce and fresh herbs. ⓐ 50 Bastion Square ⓣ 250-361-9223 ⓦ www.rebarmodernfood.com ⓒ 08.30–21.00 Mon–Wed, 08.30–22.00 Thur–Sat, 08.30–15.30 Sun

Red Fish Blue Fish ££ This eco-minded fish and chips shack, located in a bright yellow revamped shipping container on the Inner Harbour, serves OceanWise certified sustainable seafood.

📍 1006 Wharf St ☎ 250-298-6877 🌐 www.redfish-bluefish.com
🕐 11.30–19.00

AFTER DARK

RESTAURANTS

Café Brio ££ Rustic Italian with a Pacific-inflected spirit is the flavour of this kitchen. An excellent wine list and good value fixed-price menus make for an evening of fine dining with a reasonable price tag. 📍 944 Fort St ☎ 250-383-0009 🌐 www.cafe-brio.com 🕐 17.30–00.00

Zambri's ££ In an unassuming strip-mall location, this Italian kitchen has a devoted local following for its use of fresh flavours and homemade products. 📍 911 Yates St, suite 110 ☎ 250-360-1171 🌐 www.zambris.ca 🕐 11.30–14.30, 17.00–21.00 Tues–Sat

Brasserie L'Ecole £££ A charming bistro which has won Canadian and international accolades for its perfect execution and elegant presentation of everything from steak frites to local trout in browned butter. 📍 1715 Government St ☎ 250-475-6260 🌐 www.lecole.ca 🕐 17.30–23.00 Tues–Sat

Camille's Fine Westcoast Dining £££ Come to this elegant Downtown dining room for local seafood or organic game in inventive preparations, garnished with exotic wild produce such as chanterelles or salmonberries. 📍 45 Bastion Square ☎ 250-381-3433 🌐 www.camillesrestaurant.com 🕐 17.30–22.00 Tues–Sat

BARS & CLUBS

Bengal Lounge Inflected with the ambiance of colonial India, this traditional cocktail bar is the place to try Victoria gin, a locally made spirit that is always behind the bar here. There's a curry lunch and dinner buffet plus afternoon tea daily, and live jazz on Friday and Saturday nights. Located within the Fairmont Empress Hotel, an ornate chateau-style castle overlooking the harbour. ⓐ 721 Government St ⓣ 250-384-8111 ⓦ www.fairmont.com ⓛ 11.30–14.00, 18.00–23.30

Canoe Brewpub Adored for its marina-side location and spacious patio during the summer, as well as for its homemade beers (of which the signature brew is Beaver Brown Ale). The 19th-century building is the atmospheric setting for live music shows every Thursday night. ⓐ 450 Swift St ⓣ 250-361-1940 ⓦ www.canoebrewpub.com ⓛ 11.30–23.00 Sun–Wed, 11.30–00.00 Thur, 11.30–01.00 Fri & Sat

Ferris' Oyster Bar Skip the ground floor dining room and head upstairs to the oyster bar for platters of bivalves and cocktails such as Almond Cigar (aged rum, amaretto and lemon) or Saigon Presse (lime vodka, ginger, lemongrass and coriander). ⓐ 536 Yates St ⓣ 250-382-2344 ⓦ www.ferrisoysterbar.com ⓛ 16.00–01.00

Spinnaker's Brewpub & Guest House Restaurant A pub so dedicated to all things local that it bottles and sells its own aquifer mineral water, Spinnaker's also hosts wine tastings, has occasional live music performances and makes its own delicious malt vinegar. ⓐ 308 Catherine St ⓣ 250-386-2739 ⓦ www.spinnakers.com

🕐 Pub: 11.30–23.00 Mon–Fri, 11.00–23.00 Sat & Sun; store: 08.00–22.00

Veneto This upscale lounge in the newly renovated, vintage Hotel Rialto serves small tapas-style plates and inventive cocktails and martinis. 🅐 653 Pandora Ave 🕻 250-383-4157 🅦 www.hotelrialto.ca 🕐 16.00–01.00

ACCOMMODATION

Spinnakers Guest Houses £ The popular Victoria pub and restaurant (see page 125) also operates three guesthouses – a five-room Victorian 1884 Heritage Guesthouse, contemporary Garden Suites and a rustic bungalow – with reasonable rates and continental breakfast delivered from the restaurant's in-house bakery. Call for locations. 🕻 250-384-2739 🅦 www.spinnakers.com

Inn at Laurel Point ££ A little further away from Downtown, and slightly more upmarket, is this luxe resort-style hotel notable for its architectural addition by Arthur Erickson and its excellent Aura restaurant. 🅐 680 Montreal St 🕻 250-386-8721 🅦 www.laurelpoint.com

Oswego Hotel ££ Modern design-conscious comforts at nice prices, on a quiet residential street close to the harbour. 🅐 500 Oswego St 🕻 250-294-7500 🅦 www.oswegovictoria.com

▶ *Vancouver's SkyTrain on its suspended track*

PRACTICAL
information

Directory

GETTING THERE
By air

More than 60 international airlines land at YVR airport (see page 46). Among those offering direct flights from the UK are **Air Transat** (ⓦ www.airtransat.ca), **Air Canada** (ⓦ www.aircanada.com), **British Airways** (ⓦ www.britishairways.com), **Continental Airlines** (ⓦ www.continental.com), **Delta Air Lines** (ⓦ www.delta.com), **KLM** (ⓦ www.klm.com), **Lufthansa** (ⓦ www.lufthansa.com), **Northwest Airlines** (ⓦ www.nwa.com), **Thomas Cook Airlines** (ⓦ www.thomascookairlines.co.uk), **United Airlines** (ⓦ www.united.com), and **West Jet** (ⓦ www.westjet.com).

If you're visiting Vancouver Island first, a number of small aircraft and float planes fly into Victoria's airport or Downtown harbour, including **West Coast Air** (ⓦ www.westcoastair.com), **Harbour Air** (ⓦ www.harbour-air.com), **Helijet** (ⓦ www.helijet.com) and **Seair Seaplanes** (ⓦ www.seairseaplanes.com).

Many people are aware that air travel emits CO_2, which contributes to climate change. You may be interested in the possibility of lessening the environmental impact of your flight through **Climate Care** (ⓦ www.climatecare.org), which offsets your CO_2 by funding environmental projects around the world.

By rail

VIA Rail offers a variety of passes and packages that can make travelling across Canada by train economical. For example, the Canrailpass costs just $576 for 12 days of unlimited rail travel within a 30-day period. Be prepared for long rides (Edmonton to Vancouver is 27 hours by train) – for these distance journeys you'll probably want to upgrade to a sleeper or touring class ticket. The Cascades line of **Amtrak** (Ⓦ www.amtrak.com) offers trips from Vancouver all the way down to Eugene, Oregon, with the trip taking three and a half hours – just be careful you don't accidentally book a trip to or from Vancouver, Washington State in the US, by mistake! VIA Rail and Amtrak trains both arrive into Pacific Central Station (see page 51).

To take in the spectacular scenery of the Canadian Rocky Mountains from luxury carriages offering fine cuisine, choose one of the various routes offered by the **Rocky Mountaineer** (ⓐ 1775 Cottrell St ⓣ 604-606-7245 Ⓦ www.rockymountaineer.com) rail company.

⬥ *Departures hall at YVR international airport*

By road

Aside from the trusty **Greyhound** (@ 1150 Station St
@ www.greyhound.ca) bus service, **QuickShuttle**
(@ www.quickcoach.com) runs a handy, direct route from Seattle
to Vancouver, plus a shuttle from Vancouver to the Seattle
Premium Outlets mall. **Pacific Coach** (@ www.pacificcoach.com)
operates a bus service (via ferry) between the Victoria bus
terminal on Vancouver Island and Vancouver's YVR airport.

By water

If you're arriving in Vancouver via Victoria, **BC Ferries**
(@ www.bcferries.com) offers car and foot passenger options
into ferry terminals north or south of Vancouver, depending on
the route. Most major cruise ship lines pass through Vancouver
in the summer months, including Princes, Carnival, Celebrity,
Cruise West, Holland America, Norwegian, Regent, Royal
Caribbean and Silversea, most on their way to Alaska.

ENTRY FORMALITIES

Visitors from the UK and most Commonwealth countries do not
require a visa to visit Canada for stays of under six months, but
do require a valid passport. Citizens of other countries should
check with their nearest embassy before travelling. The maximum
duration of your stay will be indicated by the date stamped in
your passport by the Canadian Border Services Agency when
you pass through customs upon arriving in Canada. Information
on extending your stay is available online at @ www.cic.gc.ca.
You may be asked basic questions by a CBSA agent to ensure
you are in good health and have enough money to fund your

trip in Canada. Always have your passport, ticket and any visas or work permits with you, not in checked baggage.

When you arrive at the airport you will have to clear customs. If you are carrying camping or sports equipment, or a lot of camera or electronic apparatus, expect to have it inspected. If you are more than 19 years old, you may bring in the following amounts of duty-free goods: 1.5 litres of wine or 1.14 litres of liquor or 24 (355 millilitre) cans or bottles of beer; 200 cigarettes or 50 cigars or 200 grams of tobacco or 200 tobacco sticks. There are restrictions on various prohibited items, firearms and other weapons and on crossing the Canadian border carrying, or importing, $10,000 or more. For more information on customs regulations, see ⓦ www.cbsa.gc.ca.

MONEY

The unit of currency in Canada is the Canadian dollar ($), which is divided into 100 cents (¢). In recent years, $1 and $2 bills (notes) have been replaced with coins nicknamed the 'loonie' and 'toonie' respectively. Bills come in denominations of $5, $10, $20, $50, $100 and larger, with each bearing a different colour so they are easily distinguishable. ATMs are everywhere, and most dispense $20 bills. Note that some retailers and restaurateurs will be uneasy about accepting larger bills. Coins come in copper pennies (¢1) and (from smallest to largest, by physical size) silver-coloured dimes (¢10), nickels (¢5) and quarters (¢25). Payment via ATM card through the Interac system is frequently available and major credit cards (Visa, MasterCard, American Express) are widely accepted, including by taxis and restaurants.

In Vancouver and across British Columbia, you will pay

provincial sales tax of 7 per cent on most goods and services, including long-distance calls. Notable exceptions are food, clothing for children under 15, books and periodicals, medication and bicycles. At restaurants, a 10 per cent tax applies to alcoholic beverages and food is subject to a federal tax of 5 per cent. There are moves afoot to apply a further 7 per cent provincial sales tax to food consumed in restaurants, making a total of 12 per cent, but this was not yet confirmed at the time of writing. Hotel guests also pay a hotel tax of 8 per cent, with some areas of the province adding up to 2 per cent more in local accommodation taxes. Campsites and long-term rentals are not taxed.

HEALTH, SAFETY & CRIME

Though Vancouver is a safe city by North American standards, its rates of gun-related violent crime and property crime are among the highest in Canada. Many international gangs and crime syndicates are known to operate in Vancouver, which, because of its proximity to the US border, remains a major drug portal. Visitors are advised to take the same precautions as in any city: keep a photocopy of your passport (or email it to yourself); keep cash, documents and valuables in a secure location; avoid flashing expensive goods around in public places; store valuable items in hotel safes; don't carry large sums of cash. Vancouver's Downtown Eastside, a poor neighbourhood where many drug users gather, is to be avoided, in particular East Hastings Street from around Abbott and Carrall Streets eastwards to Commercial Drive.

The Vancouver Police Department patrols the city and, as well as dealing with emergencies and 911 calls, operates Community Policing Centres around the city.

Vancouver tap water is safe to drink, though bottled water is readily available. Medical emergencies can be handled at hospital emergency rooms and drop-in clinics (see page 138), but treatment is expensive so be sure to obtain personal medical insurance before travelling to Canada. Note that smoking is generally not permitted in public places, restaurants or bars and pubs. Look for designated smoking areas.

OPENING HOURS

Most stores and supermarkets are open by 09.00, closing around 18.00 on weekdays, or sometimes as late as 21.00 from Thursday to Saturday. On Sundays, many are open 12.00 to 17.00 or 18.00. Busier neighbourhoods have 24-hour grocery stores and pharmacies. Note that some museums and restaurants are closed on Mondays.

TOILETS

Vancouver has eight self-contained, automated public toilet kiosks in convenient locations around the city. They are free and open 24/7, and usually reasonably clean. There are also free public toilets in most parks, at public beaches and in community centres. If you're caught short in Downtown, as long as you're nicely dressed a quick foray into most hotel lobbies will yield a clean, peaceful loo. Public libraries and ubiquitous Starbucks locations are also a good bet.

CHILDREN

Vancouver sidewalks are crowded with baby strollers that are the luxe equivalent of an SUV. Fashionable neighbourhoods are chock-a-block with stylish parents with kiddies in tow, and in few places – except perhaps bars and fine-dining restaurants – will anyone look askance if you have a quiet, well-behaved child. (Minors are not allowed in nightclubs serving alcohol.) Baby products such as nappies are readily available in pharmacies and supermarkets.

Neighbourhoods like Kitsilano are rife with kiddie boutiques like **Crocodile** (ⓐ 2156 W 4th Ave ❶ 604-742-2762 ⓦ www.crocodilebaby.com ❶ 10.00–18.00) and **Hip Baby** (ⓐ 2110 W 4th Ave ❶ 604-736-8020 ⓦ www.hipbaby.com ❶ 10.00–18.00). In terms of child-friendly restaurants, Kitsilano's **Rocky Mountain Flatbread Co.** (ⓐ 1876 W 1st Ave ❶ 604-730-0231 ⓦ www.rockymountainflatbread.ca ❶ 11.30–21.30 Sun–Wed, 11.30–22.00 Thur–Sat) and, in the Commercial Drive area, **Little Nest** (ⓐ 1716 Charles St ❶ 604-251-9994 ⓦ www.littlenest.ca), are among the best.

One favourite family destination in Vancouver is **Science World** (ⓐ 1455 Quebec St ❶ 604-443-7443 ⓦ www.scienceworld.bc.ca ⓝ SkyTrain: Science World-Main Street), which you can reach from Granville Island by water taxi for extra fun factor. The **Kids Market** (ⓐ 1496 Cartwright St ❶ 604-689-8447 ⓦ www.kidsmarket.ca ❶ 10.00–18.00 ⓝ Bus: 50) at Granville Island offers two storeys of toy stores, games, food and crafts, including a ball-filled play area and an old train caboose to explore.

COMMUNICATIONS
Internet
Canadians are among the highest per-capita users of the internet in the world. Nearly all hotels offer internet access, either via a

cable in the rooms or wirelessly; as often as not, however, there is a daily charge. There's WiFi almost everywhere in the city, though increasingly it's through paid hotspot access controlled by telecommunications companies. Many cafés offer free WiFi, and the local *Province* newspaper (ⓦ www.theprovince.com) maintains an online map of free hotspots.

Phone

Phone numbers in Vancouver have ten digits, all of which must be dialled even when making a local call. When making a long-distance phone call outside of the Vancouver metropolitan area, dial 1 before the ten-digit number. In many hotels and businesses, you must dial 9 before making an outgoing call. 1-800 and 1-888 numbers are usually toll-free. For directory enquiries within the Vancouver area, call ⓣ 411.

Mobile phones use CDMA and GSM and operate on 800, 850

TELEPHONING CANADA

To call Canada from abroad, dial your country's international calling code (oo from the UK) followed by 1 and the ten-digit number you wish to call.

TELEPHONING ABROAD

To make an international call from Canada, dial 011 followed by the country code, area code (usually dropping the first 'o' if there is one) and the local number you wish to call. Country codes include: UK 44, Republic of Ireland 353, USA 1, Australia 61, New Zealand 64 and South Africa 27.

and 1900 MHz frequency ranges. Even if your phone can read the Canadian frequencies, it still may need a new SIM card, which you can buy for about $20 from major providers like Fido, Sprint and Rogers.

Post
Canada Post is reliable for both domestic and international mail. Post boxes are bright red and located on most major streets. Books of stamps can be purchased at pharmacies, newsstands and grocery stores, but for individual stamps you will need to visit a post office. See www.canadapost.com to locate your nearest post office, or ask at your hotel. Mail takes 3–5 days to reach destinations within Canada, and a week or more to send abroad.

ELECTRICITY
Electricity in Canada is 110 volts AC, 60 Hz. Plugs are the same as in the United States, two flat parallel pins with a third, round prong for grounded devices only. You can buy adapters at airports or hardware stores and borrow them from many hotel concierge desks or business centres.

TRAVELLERS WITH DISABILITIES
Vancouver started to bill itself as one of the world's most accessible cities in recent years when former mayor Sam Sullivan, a quadriplegic, was in office. Most sidewalks have lowered kerbs for wheelchairs and most attractions and hotels have accessible ramps and walkways. Many hotels offer accessible rooms with more space and adapted bathrooms. SkyTrains and SeaBuses are wheelchair-accessible and major bus routes feature 'kneeling'

buses, with ramps that descend to allow wheelchair users to enter independently. Pedestrian crossings have audible signals for visually impaired pedestrians. A Government of Canada resource, **Access to Travel** (📞 800-465-7735 🌐 www.accesstotravel.gc.ca), provides a good overview of facilities in Canada for travellers with disabilities.

TOURIST INFORMATION
Tourism Vancouver Visitor Centre 📍 200 Burrard St, plaza level 📞 604-683-2000 🌐 www.tourismvancouver.com 🕐 08.30–18.00 🚇 SkyTrain: Burrard; bus: 50, 6

BACKGROUND READING
City of Glass by Douglas Coupland. The author and artist's love letter to his home city. His seminal novel *Generation X: Tales for an Accelerated Culture*, though not actually set in Vancouver, is also a must-read.

Do Androids Dream of Electric Sheep? by Philip K Dick. Some speculate that this novel, the basis for the film *Blade Runner*, was inspired by the author's 1972 stay in a rehab facility in Vancouver.

Pattern Recognition by William Gibson. Get a taste for the futuristic work of this Vancouver-based novelist.

Stanley Park by Timothy Taylor. A prescient take on the city's growing mania for local, sustainable cuisine and a lyric rumination on its beloved green space.

Emergencies

For emergency police, ambulance and fire service, call the
toll-free number ☎ 911. You can also dial ☎ 0 to get operator
assistance.

MEDICAL SERVICES

For emergencies or to call an ambulance, dial ☎ 911. For minor
ailments, you can go to a clinic. Find a complete listing on
Vancouver Coastal Health (☎ 604-736-2033 ⓦ www.vch.ca).

Centrally located hospitals include:

St Paul's Hospital 📍 1081 Burrard St ☎ 604-682-2344
ⓦ www.providencehealthcare.org

🔺 *Vancouver police patrol car*

UBC Hospital ⓐ 2211 Westbrook Mall ❶ 604-822-7121
Ⓦ www.vch.ca
Vancouver General Hospital ⓐ 855 W 12th Ave ❶ 604-875-4111
Ⓦ www.vch.ca

POLICE

For emergency police calls, dial ❶ 911. If you need to contact the police for any other reason, use ❶ 604-717-3321. If you a victim of theft or assault, go to the nearest police station to make a report and be sure to get a copy for insurance purposes. If the problem is serious, make sure you tell them you are a foreign visitor to Vancouver and ask to speak with consular or diplomatic personnel from your home country.

EMBASSIES & CONSULATES

Australia Consulate ⓐ 1075 Georgia St W, Suite 2050
❶ 604-684-1177 Ⓦ www.ahc-ottawa.org
New Zealand Consulate General ⓐ 888 Dunsmuir St, Suite 1200
❶ 604-684-7388 Ⓦ www.nzembassy.com ❷ 08.30–16.30
Republic of Ireland Consulate ⓐ 837 Beatty St ❶ 604-683-9233
Ⓦ www3.telus.net/irishconsul
South Africa Consulate ⓐ 1075 Georgia St W, Suite 1700
❶ 604-609-3090 Ⓦ www.southafrica-canada.ca
UK Consulate General ⓐ 1111 Melville St, Suite 800
❶ 604-683-4421 Ⓦ http://ukincanada.fco.gov.uk ❷ 08.30–12.30
US Consulate General ⓐ 1075 W Pender St ❶ 604-685-4311
Ⓦ www.consular.canada.usembassy.gov ❷ 09.00–12.30 Mon–Fri

A

accommodation 32–7
    Victoria 126
    Whistler 115
air travel 46–50, 116, 128
Antique Row 118–19
Art Gallery of
    Greater Victoria 119
Arts Club Theatre 81
arts *see* culture

B

background reading 137
bars & clubs
    see nightlife
beaches 31
Bill Reid Gallery 62–4
boat travel 54, 116, 130
bus travel 46–54, 56,
    104–8, 116, 130
Butchart Gardens 119

C

cafés
    Downtown 67–9
    East Side 99–100
    Victoria 122–4
    West Side 84–6
    Whistler 112–13
car hire 56
Catriona Jeffries
    Gallery 94
children 133–4
Chinatown 58–62
cinemas 45, 89, 115

climate 8
crime 132
culture 18–20
customs & duty 131

D

disabled travellers 136–7
Downtown 58–73
driving 51–4, 56, 104

E

East Side 90–102
Eastside Cultural
    Centre 94
electricity 136
Elliot Louis Gallery 94
embassies &
    consulates 139
emergencies 138–9
entertainment 28–9
    see also nightlife
events & festivals 8–11

F

False Creek 74–8
First Nations 109
float planes 116
food & drink 24–7

G

Gallery Row 81–2
Granville Island 80
Granville Island
    Brewing 78

H

health 132–3, 138–9
Heritage Hall 96

history 14–15
hotels *see*
    accommodation
HR MacMillan
    Space Centre 44

I

internet 134–5

K

Kitsilano Beach
    & Pool 78–9

L

lifestyle 16–17
listings 20
Lululemon 23

M

Maritime Museum 44
Maritime Museum
    of British Columbia 121
markets 23, 96, 109–11
Miraj Hammam
    Spa 79–80
money 131–2
Museum of
    Anthropology 82
music 18, 28, 94

N

nightlife 28–9
    Downtown 72–3
    East Side 102
    Victoria 125–6
    West Side 88
    Whistler 114–15

O

opening hours 133

P

passports & visas 130–1

Peak 2 Peak Gondola 108

phones 135–6

police 139

Portobello
   West Market 96

post 136

public holidays 11

public transport 46–54,
   56, 104, 128–30

R

rail travel 46, 51, 104, 128–9

restaurants
   Downtown 69–72
   East Side 100–1
   Victoria 124
   West Side 86–8
   Whistler 113–14

Royal BC Museum 121

S

safety 132–3

SeaBus 56

seasons 8

Shangri-La Hotel 44, 62

shopping 22–3
   Downtown 64–7
   East Side 96–9
   Victoria 121–2
   West Side 82–4
   Whistler 112

SkyTrain 46

Solarice Spa 108

sport & activities 30–1

Squamish Lil'Wat
   Cultural Centre 111

Stanley Park 12–13

symbols &
   abbreviations 4

T

taxis 50

theatre 18–20, 81–2

time difference 46

tipping 27

toilets 133

tourist information 137

tours 111

Trout Lake 90

V

Vancouver Aquarium 44

Vancouver Art Gallery 64

Vancouver
   Convention Centre 62

Vancouver Lookout 39

Vancouver Museum 44

Vancouver Public
   Library 64

Vancouver Specials
   tour 90–4

Vancouver TheatreSports
   League 82

Vanier Park 81

Victoria 116–26

W

water taxis 74–5, 80

weather 8, 44–5

West Side 74–89

whale-watching 118

Whistler 104–15

Whistler Bike Park 108–9

Whistler Farmers'
   Market 109–11

Whistler Museum
   & Archives 111

wine & culinary tours 118

Z

Ziptrek Ecotours 111

Thomas Cook pocket guides

PARIS

Your travelling companion since 1873

Thomas
Cook